A paradox can be defined as an unacceptable conclusion derived by apparently acceptable reasoning from apparently acceptable premises. Unlike party puzzles or brain teasers, many paradoxes are serious: they raise deep philosophical problems and are associated with crises of thought and revolutionary advances. To grapple with them is not merely to engage in an intellectual game, but to come to grips with issues of real import.

The second, revised edition of this intriguing book expands and updates the text to take account of new work. It provides a valuable and accessible introduction to a range of paradoxes and their possible solutions, offers question designed to engage the reader with the arguments, and includes full bibliographic references to both classic and current literature.

"An excellent introduction to logical reasoning ... Its clarity and its non-technicality, combined with the great rigour of its treatment, make this book a small gem." Pascal Engel

PARADOXES

Second edition

PARADOXES

Second edition

R. M. SAINSBURY

CAMBRIDGE
UNIVERSITY PRESS

Published by the Press Syndicate of the University of Cambridge
The Pitt Building, Trumpington Street, Cambridge CB2 1RP
40 West 20th Street, New York, NY 10011–4211, USA
10 Stamford Road, Oakleigh, Melbourne 3166, Australia

First published 1987
Second edition 1995
Reprinted 1996

Printed in Great Britain at the University Press, Cambridge

A catalogue record for this book is available from the British Library

Library of Congress cataloging-in-publication data applied for

ISBN 0 521 48284 4   hardback
ISBN 0 521 48347 6   paperback

AU

Contents

Foreword to second edition

The main changes in this edition (apart from the correction of many typographic errors and stylistic infelicities) concern chapters 2, 5 and 6. I found my earlier discussion of vagueness very unsatisfactory, in the main because it defined vagueness in such a way as to exclude the epistemic theory. I do not accept this theory, but Timothy Williamson has shown me that I am not able to refute a skilful and determined opponent. Making room for the theory involved some quite widespread changes, including the insertion of three new sections.

The present version of chapter 5 is better structured, and there is also a change of emphasis. It now seems to me that although some kind of indexicality is involved in the Liar paradox, it is more plausible to locate this in the subject term (in the nature of self-reference) than in the predicate (by means of an indexical truth hierarchy).

The original version of chapter 6 offered a very superficial criticism of dialetheism. In those days, discussing this topic at all seemed quite adventurous. It is a tribute to dialetheists, and in particular to Graham Priest, that nowadays a book on paradoxes which did not discuss dialetheism would be clearly defective. In this edition, I offer a somewhat more extended, and I hope better, discussion, drawing in particular on a recent exchange between Timothy Smiley and Graham Priest. I find myself, to my regret, in the same frustrating position with respect to dialetheism as to the epistemic theory of vagueness: I do not accept it but cannot refute it.

In this edition, bibliographical notes have been placed at the end of the relevant chapter. Footnotes are exclusively questions for the reader.

I would like to thank many people for pointing out mistakes of varying degrees of magnitude in the first edition, either in their reviews or in personal communications: Laurence Goldstein,

Anthony Grayling, Masaki Ichinose, Frank Jackson, Anne Kelleher, Bernard Linsky, Vincent Müller, Graham Priest, Robert Seth-Smith and Roy Sorensen. I fear the list may, through inadvertence, be less than comprehensive, and I ask forgiveness of anyone whom I have omitted.

Introduction

Paradoxes are fun. In most cases, they are easy to state and immediately provoke one into trying to "solve" them.

One of the hardest paradoxes to handle is also one of the easiest to state: the Liar Paradox. One version of it asks you to consider the man who simply says, "What I am now saying is false". Is what he says true or false? The problem is that if he speaks truly, he is truly saying that what he says is false, so he is speaking falsely; but if he is speaking falsely, then, since this is just what he says he is doing, he must be speaking truly. So if what he says is false, it is true; and if it is true, it is false. This paradox is said to have "tormented many ancient logicians and caused the premature death of at least one of them, Philetas of Cos". Fun can go too far.

Paradoxes are serious. Unlike party puzzles and teasers, which are also fun, paradoxes raise serious problems. Historically, they are associated with crises in thought and with revolutionary advances. To grapple with them is not merely to engage in an intellectual game, but is to come to grips with key issues. In this book, I report some famous paradoxes and indicate how one might respond to them. These responses lead into some rather deep waters.

This is what I understand by a paradox: an apparently unacceptable conclusion derived by apparently acceptable reasoning from apparently acceptable premises. Appearances have to deceive, since the acceptable cannot lead by acceptable steps to the unacceptable. So, generally, we have a choice: either the conclusion is not really unacceptable, or else the starting point, or the reasoning, has some non-obvious flaw.

Paradoxes come in degrees, depending on how well appearance camouflages reality. Let us pretend that we can represent how paradoxical something is on a ten-point scale. The weak or shallow end we shall label 1; the cataclysmic end, home of paradoxes that send seismic shudders through a wide region of thought, we shall label 10. Serving as a marker for the point labelled 1 is the so-called Barber paradox: in a certain remote Sicilian village, approached by a long ascent up a precipitous mountain road, the barber shaves all and only those villagers who do not shave themselves. Who shaves the barber? If he himself does, then he does not (since he shaves *only* those who do not shave themselves); if he does not, then he indeed does (since he shaves *all* those who do not shave themselves). The unacceptable supposition is that there is such a barber – one who shaves himself if and only if he does not. The story may have sounded acceptable: it turned our minds, agreeably enough, to the mountains of inland Sicily. However, once we see what the consequences are, we realize that the story cannot be true: there cannot be such a barber, or such a village. The story is unacceptable. This is not a very deep paradox because the unacceptability is very thinly disguised by the mountains and the remoteness.

At the other end of the scale, the point labelled 10, I shall place the Liar. This placing seems the least that is owed to the memory of Philetas.

The deeper the paradox, the more controversial is the question of how one should respond to it. All the paradoxes I discuss in the ensuing chapters score 6 or higher on the scale, so they are really serious. (Some of those in Appendix I should, I think, score lower.) This means that there is severe and unresolved disagreement about how one should deal with them. In many cases, though certainly not all (not, for example, in the case of the Liar), I have a definite view; but I must emphasize that, although I naturally think my own view is correct, other and greater men have held views that are diametrically opposed. To get a feel for how controversial some of the issues are, I suggest examining the bibliographical notes at the ends of chapters.

Some paradoxes collect naturally into groups by subject matter. The paradoxes of Zeno which I discuss form a group because they all deal with space, time and infinity. The paradoxes of chapter 3 form a group because they bear upon the notion of rational action. Some groupings are controversial. Thus Russell grouped the paradox about classes with the Liar paradox. In the nineteen twenties, Ramsey argued that this grouping disguised a major difference. More recently, it has been argued that Russell was closer to the truth than Ramsey.

I have compared some of the paradoxes treated within a single chapter, but I have made no attempt to portray larger patterns.

However, it is arguable that there are such patterns, or even that the many paradoxes are the many signs of one "master cognitive flaw". This last claim has been ingeniously argued by Roy Sorensen (1988).

Footnotes contain questions (though not necessarily in the first sentence). I hope that considering these will give pleasure and will prompt the reader to elaborate some of the themes in the text. Asterisked footnotes are referred to in Appendix II, where I have made a point that might be relevant to an answer.

I feel that chapter 5 is the hardest and should be left until last. The first is probably the easiest. The order of the middle three is arbitrary. Chapter 6 does not introduce a paradox, but rather examines the assumption, made in the earlier chapters, that all contradictions are unacceptable. I think it would not make much sense to one completely unfamiliar with the topics discussed in chapter 5.

I face a dilemma: I find a book disappointing if the author does not express his own beliefs. What holds him back from stating, and arguing for, the truth as he sees it? I could not bring myself to exercise this restraint. On the other hand, I certainly would not want anyone to believe what I say without first carefully considering the alternatives. So I must offer somewhat paradoxical advice: be very sceptical about the proposed "solutions"; they are, I believe, correct.

1. Zeno's paradoxes: space, time, and motion

1.1 Introduction

Zeno the Greek lived in Elea (a town in what is now southern Italy) in the fifth century B.C. The paradox for which he is best known today concerns Achilles and a tortoise. For some reason now lost in the folds of time, a race was arranged between them. Since Achilles could run much faster than the tortoise, the tortoise was given a head start. Zeno's astonishing contribution is a "proof" that Achilles could never catch up with the tortoise no matter how fast he ran and no matter how long the race went on.

The supposed proof goes like this. The first thing Achilles has to do is to get to the place from which the tortoise started. The tortoise, although slow, is unflagging: while Achilles is occupied in making up his handicap, the tortoise advances a little bit further. So the next thing Achilles has to do is to get to the *new* place the tortoise occupies. While he is doing this, the tortoise will have gone on a little bit further still. However small the gap that remains, it will take Achilles some time to cross it, and in that time the tortoise will have created another gap. So however fast Achilles runs, all the tortoise need do in order not to be beaten is keep going – to make *some* progress in the time it takes Achilles to close the previous gap between them.

No one nowadays would dream of accepting the conclusion that Achilles cannot catch the tortoise. (I will not vouch for Zeno's reaction to his paradox: sometimes he is reported as having taken his paradoxical conclusions quite seriously and literally, showing that motion was impossible.) Therefore, there must be something wrong with the argument. Saying exactly *what* is wrong is not easy, and there is no uncontroversial diagnosis. Some have seen the paradox as produced by the assumption that space or time is infinitely divisible, and thus as genuinely proving that space or time is *not* infinitely divisible. Others have seen in the argument nothing more than a display of ignorance of elementary mathematics – an ignorance perhaps excusable in Zeno's time but inexcusable today.

The paradox of Achilles and the tortoise is Zeno's most famous, but there were several others. The Achilles paradox takes for granted that Achilles can start running, and purports to prove that he cannot get as far as we all know he can. This paradox dovetails nicely with one known as the Racetrack, or Dichotomy, which purports to show that nothing can *begin* to move. In order to get anywhere, say to a point one foot ahead of you, you must first get halfway there. To get to the halfway point, you must first get halfway to *that* point. In short, in order to get anywhere, even to begin to move, you must first perform an infinity of other movements. Since this seems impossible, it seems impossible that anything should move at all.

Almost none of Zeno's work survives as such. For the most part, our knowledge of what his arguments were is derived from reports by other philosophers, notably Aristotle. He presents Zeno's arguments very briefly, no doubt in the expectation that they would be familiar to his audience from the oral tradition that was perhaps his own only source. Aristotle's accounts are so compressed that only by guesswork can one reconstruct a detailed argument. The upshot is that there is no universal agreement about what should count as "Zeno's paradoxes", or about exactly what his arguments were. I shall select arguments that I believe to be interesting and important, and which are commonly attributed to Zeno, but I make no claim to be expounding what the real, historical Zeno actually said or thought.

Aristotle is an example of a great thinker who believed that Zeno was to be taken seriously and not dismissed as a mere propounder of childish riddles. By contrast, Charles Peirce wrote of the Achilles paradox:

> this ridiculous little catch presents no difficulty at all to a mind adequately trained in mathematics and in logic, but is one of those which is very apt to excite minds of a certain class to an obstinate determination to believe a given proposition. (1935, vol. 6, §177, p. 122)

On balance, history has sided with Aristotle, whose view on this point has been shared by thinkers as dissimilar as Hegel and Russell.

I shall discuss three Zenonian paradoxes concerning motion: the Racetrack, the Achilles, and a paradox known as the Arrow. Before doing so, however, it will be useful to consider yet another of Zeno's paradoxes, one that concerns space. Sorting out this paradox provides the groundwork for tackling the paradoxes of motion.

1.2 Space

In ancient times, a frequently discussed perplexity was how something ("one and the same thing") could be both one and many. For example, a book is one but also many (words or pages); likewise, a tree is one but also many (leaves, branches, molecules, or whatever). Nowadays, this is unlikely to strike any-one as very problematic. When we say that the book or the tree *is* many things, we do not mean that it is identical with many things (which would be absurd), but rather that it is made up of many parts. Furthermore, at least on the face of it, there is nothing espe-cially problematic about this relationship between a whole and the parts which compose it.[1]

Zeno, like his teacher Parmenides, wished to argue that in such cases there are not many things but only one thing. I shall ex-amine one ingredient of this argument. Consider any region of space, for example the region occupied by this book. The region can be thought of as having parts which are themselves spatial, that is, they have some size. This holds however small we make the parts. Hence, the argument runs, no region of space is "infinitely divisible" in the sense of containing an *infinite* number of spatial parts. For each part has a size, and a region composed of an infinite number of parts of this size must be infinite in size.

This argument played the following role in Zeno's attempt to show that it is not the case that there are "many things". He was talking only of objects in space, and he assumed that an object has a part corresponding to every part of the space it fills. He claimed to show that, if you allow that objects have parts at all, you must say that each object is infinitely large, which is absurd. You must therefore deny that objects have parts. From this he went on to

---

1 Appearances may deceive. Let us call some particular tree T, and the collection of its parts at a particular moment P. Since trees can survive the loss of some of their parts (e.g., of their leaves in the fall), T can exist when P no longer does. Does this mean that T is something other than P or, more generally, that each thing is distinct from the sum of its parts? Can P exist when T does not (e.g., if the parts of the tree are dispersed by timber-felling operations)?

argue that *plurality* – the existence of many things – was impossible. I shall not consider this further development, but will instead return to the argument against infinite divisibility upon which it draws.[2]

The conclusion may seem surprising. Surely one could convince oneself that any space has infinitely many spatial parts. Suppose we take a rectangle and bisect it vertically to give two further rectangles. Taking the right-hand one, bisect it vertically to give two more new rectangles. Cannot this process of bisection go on indefinitely, at least in theory? If so, any spatial area is made up of infinitely many others.

Wait one moment! Suppose that I am drawing the bisections with a ruler and pencil. However thin the pencil, the time will fairly soon come when, instead of producing fresh rectangles, the new lines will fuse into a smudge. Alternatively, suppose that I am cutting the rectangles from paper with scissors. Again, the time will fairly soon come when my strip of paper will be too small to cut. More scientifically, such a process of physical division must presumably come to an end *sometime*: at the very latest, when the remainder of the object is no more than an atom (proton, hadron, quark, or whatever) wide.

The proponent of infinite divisibility must claim to have no such physical process in mind, but rather to be presenting a purely intellectual process: for every rectangle we can consider, we can also consider a smaller one having half the width. This is how we conceive any space, regardless of its shape. What we have to discuss, therefore, is whether the earlier argument demonstrates that space cannot be as we tend to conceive it; whether, that is, the earlier argument succeeded in showing that no region could have infinitely many parts.

We all know that there are finite spaces which have spatial parts, but the argument supposedly shows that there are not. Therefore we must reject one of the premises that leads to this absurd conclusion, and the most suitable for rejection, because it is the most controversial, is that space is infinitely divisible. This premise supposedly forces us to say that either the parts of a supposedly infinitely divisible space are finite in size, or they are not. If the latter holds, then they are nothing, and no number of them could together compose a finite space. If the former holds, infinitely many of them together will together compose an infinitely large space. Either way, on the supposition that space is infinitely

2*   Given as a premise that no object has parts, how could one attempt to argue that there is no more than one object?

divisible, there are no finite spaces. Since there obviously are finite spaces, the supposition must be rejected.

The notion of infinite divisibility remains ambiguous. On the one hand, to say that any space is infinitely divisible could mean that there is no upper limit to the number of imaginary operations of dividing we could effect. On the other hand, it could mean that the space contains an infinite number of parts. It is not obvious that the latter follows from the former. The latter claim might seem to rely on the idea that the process of imaginary dividings could somehow be "completed". For the moment let us assume that the thesis of infinite divisibility at stake is the thesis that space contains infinitely many non-overlapping parts, and that each part has some finite size.

The most doubtful part of the argument against the thesis is the claim that a space composed of an infinity of parts, each finite in size, must be infinite. This claim is incorrect, and one way to show it is to appeal to mathematics. Let us represent the imagined successive bisections by the following series:

$$\frac{1}{2}, \frac{1}{4}, \frac{1}{8}, \ldots$$

where the first term ($\frac{1}{2}$) represents the fact that, after the first bisection, the right-hand rectangle is only half the area of the original rectangle; and similarly for the other terms. Every member of this series is a finite number, just as each of the spatial parts is of finite size. This does not mean that the sum of the series is infinite. On the contrary, mathematics texts have it that this series sums to 1. If we find nothing problematic in the idea that an infinite collection of finite numbers has a finite sum, then by analogy we should be happy with the idea that an infinite collection of finite spatial parts can compose a finite spatial region.[3]

---

3   Someone might object: is it not just a *convention* in mathematics to treat this series as summing to 1? More generally, is it not just a convention to treat the sum of an infinite series as the limit of the partial sums? If this is a mere mathematical convention, how can it tell us anything about space? Readers with mathematical backgrounds might like to comment on the following argument, which purports to show that the fact that the series sums to 1 can be derived from ordinary arithmetical notions, without appeal to any special convention. (*Warning*: mathematicians tell me that what follows is highly suspect!)
The series can be represented as
$$x + x^2 + x^3 + \ldots$$
where $x = \frac{1}{2}$. Multiplying this expression by x has the effect of lopping off the first term:
$$x(x + x^2 + x^3 + \ldots) = x^2 + x^3 + x^4 + \ldots$$

This argument from mathematics establishes the analogous point about space (namely, that infinitely many parts of finite size may together form a finite whole) only upon the assumption that the analogy is good: that space, in the respect in question, has the properties that numbers have. However, this is controversial. For example, we have already said that some people take Zeno's paradoxes to show that space is not continuous, although the series of numbers is. Hence we would do well to approach the issue again. We do not have to rely on any mathematical argument to show that a finite whole can be composed of an infinite number of finite parts.

There are two rather similar propositions, one true and one false, and we must be careful not to confuse them.

(1)   If, for some finite size, a whole contains infinitely many parts none smaller than this size, then the whole is infinitely large.

(2)   If a whole contains infinitely many parts, each of some finite size, then the whole is infinitely large.

Statement (1) is true. To see this, let the minimum size of the parts be δ (say linear or square or cubic inches). Then the size of the whole is $\infty \times \delta$, which is clearly an infinite number. However, (1) does not bear on the case we are considering. To see this, let us revert to our imagined bisections. The idea was that however small the remaining area was, we could always imagine it being divided into two. This means that there can be no lower limit on how small the parts are. There can be no size δ such that all the parts are at least this big. For any such size, we can always imagine it being divided into two.

To see that (2) is false, we need to remember that it is essential to the idea of infinite divisibility that the parts get smaller, without limit, as the imagined process of division proceeds. This gives us an almost visual way of understanding how the endless series

---

Here we apply a generalization of the principle of distribution:
$$a.(b + c) = (a.b) + (a.c).$$
Using this together with a similar generalization of the principle that
$$(1-a).(b + c) = (b + c) - a.(b + c)$$
we get:
$$(1-x).(x + x^2 + x^3 + \ldots) = (x + x^2 + x^3 + \ldots) - (x^2 + x^3 + x^4 + \ldots)$$
Thus
$$(1-x).(x + x^2 + x^3 + \ldots) = x$$
So, dividing both sides by $(1-x)$:
$$x + x^2 + x^3 + \ldots = \frac{x}{(1-x)}$$
So where $x = \frac{1}{2}$, the sum of the series is equal to 1.

of rectangles can fit into the original rectangle: by getting progressively smaller.

It would be as wrong to infer "There is a finite size which every part possesses" from "Every part has some finite size or other" as it would be to infer "There is a woman who is loved by every man" from "Every man loves some woman or other". (Readers trained in formal logic will recognize a quantifier-shift fallacy here: one cannot infer an $\exists\forall$ conclusion from the corresponding $\forall\exists$ premise.)

The explanation for any tendency to believe that (2) is true lies in a tendency to confuse it with (1). We perhaps tend to think: *at the end of the series* the *last* pair of rectangles formed have some finite size, and all the other infinitely many rectangles are larger. Therefore, taken together they must make up an infinite area. However, there is *no such thing* as the last pair of rectangles to be formed: our infinite series of divisions has no last member. Once we hold clearly in mind that there can be no lower limit on the size of the parts induced by the infinite series of envisaged divisions, there is no inclination to suppose that having infinitely many parts entails being infinitely large.

The upshot is that there is no contradiction in the idea that space is infinitely divisible, in the sense of being composed of infinitely many non-overlapping spatial parts, each of some finite (non-zero) size. This does not establish that space *is* infinitely divisible. Perhaps it is granular, in the way in which, according to quantum theory, energy is. Perhaps there are small spatial regions that have no distinct sub-regions. The present point, however, is that the Zenonian argument we have discussed gives us no reason at all to believe this granular hypothesis.

This supposed paradox about space may well not strike us as very deep, especially if we have some familiarity with the currently orthodox mathematical treatment of infinity. Still, we must not forget that current orthodoxy was not developed without struggle, and was achieved several centuries after Zeno had pondered these questions. Zeno and his contemporaries might with good reason have had more trouble with it than we do. The position of a paradox on the ten-point scale mentioned in the Introduction can change over time: as we become more sophisticated detectors of mere appearance, a paradox can slide down toward the Barber end of the scale.

Clearing this paradox out of the way will prove to have been an essential preliminary to discussing Zeno's deeper paradoxes, which concern motion.

1.3   The Racetrack

If a runner is to reach the end of the track, he must first complete an infinite number of different journeys: getting to the mid-point, then to the point midway between the midpoint and the end, then to the point midway between this one and the end, and so on. Since it is logically impossible for someone to complete an infinite series of journeys, the runner cannot reach the end of the track. It is irrelevant how far away the end of the track is – it could be just a few inches away – so this argument, if sound, will show that all motion is impossible. Moving to any point will involve an infinite number of journeys, and an infinite number of journeys cannot be completed.

Let us call the starting point Z (for Zeno), and the endpoint Z^*. The argument can be analysed into two premises and a conclusion, as follows:

(1)   Going from Z to Z^* would require one to complete an infinite number of journeys: from Z to the point midway to Z^*, call it Z_1; from Z_1 to the point midway between it and Z^*, call it Z_2; and so on.

(2)   It is logically impossible for anyone (or anything) to complete an infinite number of journeys.

Conclusion: It is logically impossible for anyone to go from Z to Z^*. Since these points are arbitrary, *all* motion is impossible.

Apparently acceptable premises, (1) and (2), lead by apparently acceptable reasoning to an apparently unacceptable conclusion.

No one nowadays would for a moment entertain the idea that the conclusion is, despite appearances, acceptable. (I refrain from vouching for Zeno's own response.) Moreover, the reasoning appears impeccable. So for us the question is this: which premise is incorrect, and why?

Let us begin by considering premise (1). The idea is that we can generate an infinite series, let us call it the Z-series, whose terms are

$$Z, Z_1, Z_2, \dots .$$

These terms, it is proposed, can be used to analyse the journey from Z to Z^*, for they are among the points that a runner from Z to Z^* must pass through en route. However, Z^* itself is not a term in the series; that is, it is not generated by the operation that generates new terms in the series – halving the distance that remains between the previous term and Z^*.

The word "journey" has, in the context, some misleading implications. Perhaps "journey" connotes an event done with certain intentions, but it is obvious that a runner could form no intention with respect to most of the members of Z-series, for he would have neither the time, nor the memory, nor the conceptual apparatus to think about most of them. Furthermore, he may well form no intention with respect to those he *can* think about. Still, if we explicitly set these connotations aside, then (1) seems hard to deny, once the infinite divisibility of space is granted; for then all (1) means is the apparent platitude that motion from Z to Z* involves traversing the distances Z to Z_1, Z_1 to Z_2, and so on.

Suspicion focuses on (2). Why should one not be able to complete an infinite number of journeys in a finite time? Is that not precisely what *does* happen when anything moves? Furthermore, is it not something that *could* happen even in other cases? For example, consider a view that Bertrand Russell once affirmed: he argued that we could imagine someone getting more and more skilful in performing a given task, and so completing it more and more quickly. On the first occasion, it might take one minute to do the job, on the second, only a half a minute, and so on, so that, performing the tasks consecutively, the whole series of infinitely many could be performed in the space of two minutes. Russell said, indeed, that this was "medically impossible" but he held that it was *logically* possible: no contradiction was involved. If Russell is right about this, then (2) is the premise we should reject.

However, consider the following argument, in which the word "task" is used in quite a general way, so as to subsume what we have been calling "journeys".

> There are certain reading-lamps that have a button in the base. If the lamp is off and you press the button the lamp goes on, and if the lamp is on and you press the button the lamp goes off.
> Suppose now that the lamp is off, and I succeed in pressing the button an infinite number of times, perhaps making one jab in one minute, another jab in the next half-minute, and so on, according to Russell's recipe. After I have completed the whole infinite sequence of jabs, i.e., at the end of two minutes, is the lamp on or off? It seems impossible to answer this question. It cannot be on, because I did not ever turn it on without at once turning it off. It cannot be off, because I did in the first place turn it on, and thereafter I never turned it off without at once turning it on. But the lamp must

be either on or off. This is a contradiction. (Thomson 1954; cited in Gale 1968, p. 411)

Let us call the envisaged set-up consisting of me, the switch, the lamp, and so on, "Thomson's lamp". The argument purports to show that Thomson's lamp cannot complete an infinite series of switchings in a finite time. It proceeds by *reductio ad absurdum*: we suppose that it *can* complete such a series, and show that this supposition leads to an absurdity – that the lamp is neither on nor off at the supposed end of the series of tasks.

The argument is not valid. The supposition that the infinite series has been completed does not lead to the absurdity that the lamp is neither on nor off. Nothing follows from this supposition about the state of the lamp *after* the infinite series of switchings.

Consider the series of moments T_1, T_2, ..., each corresponding to a switching. According to the story, the gaps between the members of this T-series get smaller and smaller, and the rate of switching increases. At T_1 a switching on occurs, at T_2 a switching off occurs, and so on. Call the first moment after the (supposed) completion of the series T^*. It follows from the specification of the infinite series that, for any moment *in the T-series*, if the lamp is on at that moment there is a later moment in the series at which the lamp is off; and vice versa. However, nothing follows from this about whether the lamp is on or off *at T^**, for T^* does *not belong* to the T-series. T^* is not generated by the operation that generates new members of the T-series from old: being a time half as remote from the old member as its predecessor was from it. The specification of the task speaks only to members of the T-series, and this has no consequences, let alone contradictory consequences, for how things are *at T^**, which lies outside the series.[4]

The preceding paragraph is not designed to prove that it is logically possible for an infinite series of tasks to be completed. It is designed to show only that Thomson's argument against this possibility fails. In fact, someone might suggest a reason of a different kind for thinking that there is a logical absurdity in the idea of Thomson's lamp.

Consider the lamp's button. We imagine it to move the same distance for each switching. If it has moved infinitely many times, then an infinite distance has been traversed at a finite speed in a finite time. There is a case for saying that this is logically impossible, for there is a case for saying that what we *mean* by average

4   Are we entitled to speak of "the first moment after the (supposed) completion of the task"?

speed is simply distance divided by total time. It follows that if speed and total time are finite, so is distance. If this is allowed, then Thomson was right to say that Thomson's lamp as he described it is a logical impossibility, even though the argument he gave for this conclusion was unsatisfactory.

This objection might be countered by varying the design of the machine. There are at least two possibilities. One is that the machine's switch be so constructed that if on its first switching it travels through a distance δ, then on the second switching it travels δ/2, on the third δ/4, and so on. Another is that the switch be so constructed that it travels faster and faster on each switching, without limit.[5,6] It is hard to find positive arguments for the conclusion that this machine is logically possible; but this machine is open neither to Thomson's objection, which was invalid, nor to the objection that it involves an infinite distance being travelled in a finite time. Therefore, until some other objection is forthcoming, we can (provisionally, and with due caution) accept this revised Thomson's lamp as a logical possibility. What's more, if *it* is a possibility, then there's nothing logically impossible about a runner completing an infinite series of journeys.[7]

One does not need to establish outré possibilities, such as that of a Thomson's lamp that can complete an infinite number of tasks, in order to establish that the runner can reach Z^*. The argument is supposed to work the other way: if even the infinite Thomson's lamp is possible, then there can be no problem about the runner.

In the next section, I discuss a rather sophisticated variant of the Racetrack. The discussion may help resolve some of the worries that remain with this paradox.

---

[5]   Does this mean that it would have to travel infinitely fast in the end?

[6*] Does this mean that the switch would have to travel faster than the speed of light? If so, does this mean that the machine is *logically* impossible?

[7]   Evaluate the following argument:
We can all agree that the series of numbers $\frac{1}{2}, \frac{1}{4}, \frac{1}{8}, \ldots$ sums to 1. What is controversial is whether this fact has any bearing on whether the runner can reach Z^*. We know that it would be absurd to say that energy is infinitely divisible merely because for any number that is used to measure some quantity of energy there is a smaller one. Likewise, Zeno's paradox of the runner shows that motion through space should not be thought of as an endless progression through an infinite series. It is as clear that there is a smallest motion a runner can make as it is that there is a smallest spatial distance that we are capable of measuring.

1.4   The Racetrack again

Premise (1) of the previous section asserted that a necessary condition of moving from Z to Z^* is moving through the infinite series of intermediate Z-points. In this rerun, I want to consider a different problem. It is that there appear to be persuasive arguments for the following inconsistent conclusions:

(a)   Passing through all the Z-points is sufficient for reaching Z^*.

(b)   Passing through all the Z-points is *not* sufficient for reaching Z^*.

We cannot accept both (a) and (b). The contradiction might be used to disprove the view that the runner's journey can be analysed in terms of an infinite series, and this would throw doubt on our earlier premise (1) (p. 12).

Let us look more closely at an argument for (a):

> Suppose someone could have occupied every point in the Z-series without having occupied any point outside it, in particular without having occupied Z^*. Where would he be? Not at any Z-point, for then there would be an unoccupied Z-point to the right. Not, for the same reason, between Z-points. And, *ex hypothesi,* not at any point external to the Z-series. But these possibilities are exhaustive. (Cf. Thomson 1954; cited in Gale 1968, p. 418)

In other words, if you pass through all the Z-points, you *must* get to Z^*. Contrasted with this is a simple argument against sufficiency – an argument for (b):

> Z^* lies outside the Z-series. It is further to the right than any member of the Z-series. So going through all the members of the Z-series cannot take you as far to the right as Z^*. So reaching Z^* is not logically entailed by passing through every Z-point.

The new twist to the Racetrack is that we have plausible arguments for both (a) and (b), but these are inconsistent.

The following objection to the argument for (a) has been proposed by Paul Benacerraf (1962, p. 774). A possible answer to the question "Where would the runner be after passing through all the Z-points?" is "Nowhere!". Passing through all the Z-points is not sufficient for arriving at Z^* because one might cease to exist after reaching every Z-point but without reaching Z^*. To lend colour to this suggestion, Benacerraf invites us to imagine a genie who "shrinks from the thought" of reaching $Z*$ – to such an extent that he gets progressively smaller as his journey progresses. By Z_1 he is half his original size, by Z_2 a quarter of it, and so on. Thus by the time he has passed through every Z-point his size is zero, and "there is not enough left of him" to occupy $Z*$.

Even if this is accepted,[8] it will not resolve our problem. The most that it could achieve is a qualification of (a). What would have to be said to be sufficient for reaching $Z*$ is not merely passing through every Z-point, but doing that and *also* (!) continuing to exist. However, the argument against sufficiency, if it is good at all, seems just as good against a correspondingly modified version of (b). Since $Z*$ lies outside the Z-series, even passing through every Z-point *and* continuing to exist cannot logically guarantee arriving at $Z*$.

Part of the puzzle here lies, I think, in the exact nature of the correspondence that we are setting up between mathematical series and physical space. We have two different things: on the one hand, a series of mathematical points, the Z-series, and on the other hand, a series of physical points composing the physical racetrack. A mathematical series, like the Z-series, may have no last member. In this case, it is not clear how we are to answer the question "To what physical length does this series of mathematical points correspond?". That this is a genuine question is obscured by the fact that we can properly apply the word "point" both to a mathematical abstraction and to a position in physical space. However, lengths as ordinarily thought of have *two* ends. If a length can be correlated with a mathematical series with only *one* end, like the Z-series, this can only be by stipulation. So if we are to think of part of the racetrack as a length, a two-ended length, corresponding to the mathematically defined Z-series, a one-ended length, we can but stipulate that what corresponds to the physical length is the series from Z to $Z*$. Given this, it is obvious that traversing the length corresponding to the Z-series is enough to get the runner to $Z*$. On this view, the paradox is resolved by rejecting the argument for (b), and accepting that for (a) – modified, perhaps, by the quibble about the runner continuing to exist.

---

[8]*   Can the following objection be met?

     Where is the runner when he goes out of existence? He cannot be at any Z-point since, by hypothesis, there is always a Z-point beyond it, which means that he would not have gone through all the Z-points; but if he goes out of existence at or beyond $Z*$, then he reached $Z*$, and so the sufficiency claim has not been refuted.

This suggestion can be strengthened by the following consideration. Suppose we divide a line into two discrete parts, X and Y, by drawing a perpendicular that cuts it at a point B:

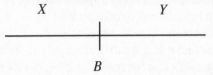

The notions of *line*, *division*, and so on are to be just our ordinary ones, whatever they are, and not some mathematical specification of them. Since B is a spatial point, it must be somewhere. So is it in X or in Y or both? We cannot say that it is in both X and Y, since by hypothesis these are discrete lines; that is, they have no point in common. However, it would seem that any reason we could have for saying that B is in X is as good a reason for saying that it is in Y. So, if it is in either, then it is in both, which is impossible.

If we try to represent the intuitive idea in the diagram in mathematically precise terms, we have to make a choice. Let us think of lengths in terms of sets of (mathematical) points. If X and Y are to be discrete (have no points in common), we must choose between assigning B to X (as its last member, in a left-to-right ordering) and assigning B to Y (as its first member). If we make the first choice, then Y has no first member; if we make the second choice, then X has no last member. So far as having an adequate model for physical space goes, there seems to be nothing to determine this choice – it seems that we are free to stipulate.

Suppose we make the first choice, according to which B is in X. Imagine an archer being asked to shoot an arrow that traverses the whole of a physical space corresponding to X, without entering into any of the space corresponding to Y. There is no conceptual problem about this instruction: the arrow must be shot from the leftmost point of X and land at B. Now imagine an archer being asked to shoot an arrow that traverses the whole of a physical space corresponding to Y, without entering into any of the space corresponding to X. This time there appears to be a conceptual problem. The arrow cannot land at the point in space corresponding to B because, by stipulation, B has been allocated to X and so lies outside Y; but nor can the arrow land anywhere in Y, since for any point in Y there is one between it and B. There is no point that is the *first* point to the right of B.

What is odd about this contrast – the ease of occupying all of X and none of Y, the difficulty of occupying all of Y and none of X – is that *which* task is problematic depends upon a stipulation. If we had made the other choice, stipulating that *B* is to belong to *Y*, the difficulties would have been transposed.

Two real physical tasks, involving physical space, cannot vary in their difficulty according to some stipulation about how *B* is to be allocated. There is some discrepancy here between the abstract mathematical space-like notions, and our notions of physical space.

If we think of *X* and *Y* as genuine lengths, as stretches of physical space, the difficulty we face can be traced to the source already mentioned: lengths – for example, the lengths of race-tracks – have *two* ends. However, if *B* belongs to *X* and not *Y*, then *Y* seems to lack a left-hand end: it cannot have *B* as its end, since *B* belongs to *X* and not *Y* (by hypothesis); but it cannot have any point to the right of *B* as its left end, for there will always be a *Y*-point to the left of any point that is to the right of *B*.

The difficulty comes from the assumption that the point *B* has partially to *compose* a line to which it belongs, so that to say it belongs to *X* and *Y* would be inconsistent with these being non-overlapping lines. For an adequate description of physical space, we need a different notion: one that allows, for example, that two distinct physical lengths, arranged like *X* and *Y*, should touch without overlapping. We need the notion of a boundary that does not itself occupy space.

If we ask what region of space – thought of in the way we think of racetracks, as having two ends – corresponds to the points on the *Z*-series, the only possible answer would appear to be the region from *Z* to *Z**. This explains why the argument for sufficiency is correct, despite the point noted in the argument against it. *Z** does not belong to the *Z*-series, but it does belong to the region of space that corresponds to the *Z*-series.

In these remarks, I have assumed that we have coherent spatial notions, for example, that of (two-ended) length, and that if some mathematical structure does not fit with these notions, then so much the worse for the view that the structure gives a correct account of our spatial notions. In the circumstances, this pattern of argument is suspect, for it is open to the following Zeno-like response: the *only* way we could hope to arrive at coherent spatial notions is through these mathematical structures. If this way fails – if the mathematical structures do not yield all we want – then we are forced to admit that we were after the impossible, that there is no way of making sense of our spatial concepts.

The upshot is that a full response to Zeno's Racetrack paradox would require a detailed elaboration and justification of our spatial concepts. This is the task Zeno set us – a task that each generation of philosophers of space and time rightly feels it must undertake anew.

1.5   Achilles and the Tortoise

We can restate this most famous of paradoxes using some Racetrack terminology. The Z-series can be redefined as follows: Z is Achilles' starting point; Z_1 is the tortoise's starting point; Z_2 is the point that the tortoise reaches while Achilles is getting to Z_1; and so on. Z^* becomes the point at which, we all believe, Achilles will catch the tortoise, and the "proof" is that Achilles, like the runner before him, will never reach Z^*.

We can see this as nothing more, in essentials, than the Racetrack, but with a receding finishing line. The paradoxical claim is this: Achilles can never get to Z^* because however many points in the Z-series he has occupied, there are still more Z-points ahead before he gets to Z^*. Furthermore, we cannot expect him to complete an infinity of "tasks" (moving through Z-points) in a finite time. An adequate response to the Racetrack will be easily converted into an adequate response to this version of the Achilles.

In such an interpretation of the paradox, the tortoise has barely a walk-on part to play. Let us see if we can do him more justice. One attempt is this:

> The tortoise is always ahead of Achilles if Achilles is at a point in the Z-series. But how is this consistent with the supposition that they reach Z^* at the same time? If the tortoise is always ahead in the Z-series, must he not emerge from it before Achilles?

This makes for a rather superficial paradox. It is trivial that the tortoise is ahead of Achilles all the time until Achilles has drawn level: he is ahead until Z^*. Given that both of them can travel through all the Z-points, which was disputed in the Racetrack but which is not now challenged, there is no reason why they should not complete this task at the same point in space and time. So I have to report that I can find nothing of substantial interest in this paradox that has not already been discussed in connection with the Racetrack.

1.6   The Arrow

At any instant of time, the flying arrow "occupies a space equal to itself". That is, the arrow at an instant cannot be moving, for motion takes a period of time, and a temporal instant is conceived as a point, not itself having duration. It follows that the arrow is at rest at every instant, and so does not move. What goes for arrows goes for everything: nothing moves.

Aristotle gives a very brief report of this paradoxical argument, and concludes that it shows that "time is not composed of indivisible instants" (*Physics*, Z9. 239b 5). This is one possible response, though one that would currently lack appeal. Classical mechanics purports to make sense not only of velocity at an instant but also of various more sophisticated notions: rate of change of velocity at an instant (i.e., instantaneous acceleration or deceleration), rate of change of acceleration at an instant, and so on.

Another response is to accept that the arrow is at rest at every instant, but deny that it follows that it does not move. What is required for the arrow to move, it may be said, is not that it move-at-an-instant, which is clearly an impossibility (given the semi-technical notion of *instant* in question), but rather that it be at different places at different instants. An instant is not long enough for motion to occur, for motion is a relation between an object, places, and various instants. If a response along these lines can be justified, there is no need to accept Aristotle's conclusion.

Suppose we set out Zeno's argument like this:

(1)   At each instant, the arrow does not move.
(2)   A stretch of time is composed of instants.
Conclusion: In any stretch of time, the arrow does not move.

Then the response under discussion is that this argument is not valid: the premises are true, but they do not entail the conclusion.

If the first premise is to be acceptable, it must be understood in a rather special way, which provides the key to the paradox. It must be understood as making a claim which does not immediately entail that the arrow is at rest. The question of whether something is moving or at rest "at an instant" is one that essentially involves other instants. An object is at rest at an instant just on condition that it is at the same place at all nearby instants; it is in motion at an instant just on condition that it is in different places at nearby instants. Nothing about the arrow and a single instant alone can fix either that it is moving then or at rest then. In short, the first premise, if acceptable, cannot be understood as saying that at each instant the arrow is at rest.

Once the first premise is properly understood, it is easy to see why the argument is fallacious. The conclusion that the arrow is always at rest says of each instant that the arrow is in the same place at neighbouring instants. No such information is contained in the premises. If we think it is implicit in the premises, this is probably because we are failing to distinguish between the claim – interpretable as true – that at each instant the arrow does not move, and the false claim that it is *at rest* at each instant.

If this is correct, then the Arrow paradox is an example of one in which the unacceptable conclusion (nothing moves) comes from an acceptable premise (no motion occurs "during" an instant) by unacceptable reasoning.

Bibliographical notes

Salmon (1970) contains the articles by Thomson (1954) and Benacerraf (1962) from which I drew the discussion of infinity machines, as well as many other important articles, including a clear introductory survey by Salmon. It also has an excellent bibliography. For a fine introduction to the philosophy of space and time, including a chapter on Zeno's paradoxes, see Salmon (1980).

For a historical account see Vlastos (1967). For an advanced discussion, see Grünbaum (1967).

The quotation from Peirce, written late in his life, is not representative. In many other places, he discusses Zeno's paradoxes very seriously. However, it is not uncommon for people to see a paradox as trivial once they think they have a definitive solution to it. The cure for this reaction is to try to persuade someone else of one's "solution".

The phrase "medically impossible" comes from Russell (1936, p. 143).

2.   Vagueness: the paradox of the heap

2.1   Sorites paradoxes: preliminaries

Suppose two people differ in height by one-tenth of an inch (0.1").
We are inclined to believe that either both or neither are tall. If one
is 6' 6" and the other is 0.1" shorter than this, then both are tall. If
one is 4' 6" and the other is 0.1" taller, then neither is tall. This apparently obvious and uncontroversial supposition appears to lead to
the paradoxical conclusion that everyone is tall. Consider a series
of heights starting with 6' 6" and descending by steps of 0.1". A
person of 6' 6" is tall. By our supposition, so must be a person of
6' 5.9". However, if a person of this height is tall, so must be a
person one-tenth of an inch smaller; and so on, without limit, until
we find ourselves forced to say, absurdly, that a 4' 6" person is
tall;[1] indeed, that everyone is tall.

In ancient times, a similar paradox was told in terms of a heap,
and a Greek word for "heap" – *soros* – has given rise to the use of
the word "sorites" for all paradoxes of this kind. Suppose you
have a heap of sand. If you take away one grain of sand, what remains is still a heap: removing a single grain cannot turn a heap
into something that is not a heap. If two collections of grains of
sand differ in number by just one grain, then both or neither are
heaps. This apparently obvious and uncontroversial supposition
appears to lead to the paradoxical conclusion that all collections of
grains of sand, even one-membered collections, are heaps.

Suppose you are looking at a spectrum of colours painted on a
wall through a device with a split window which divides the section of the spectrum you can see into two equal adjacent areas.
Suppose the spectrum is so broad and the windows so narrow that

---

[1]   How should one respond to the objection that someone 4' 6" tall may be
    tall for a pygmy?

What is the line between? [in margin]

bald + full of hair? [in margin]

There is a vagueness [in margin]

or more def. of vagueness def of [in margin]

allows both to be the same. [in margin]

the colours in the two visible windows are indistinguishable, no matter where in the spectrum the device is positioned. The device is first placed at the red end of the wall, and then moved gradually rightward to the blue end. It is moved in such a way that the area that was visible in the right-hand window in the previous position is now visible in the left. At the beginning you will unhesitatingly judge that both areas are red. At each point, the newly visible area will appear indistinguishable from an area that you have already judged to be red and that is still visible. One feels bound by the principle that if two coloured patches are indistinguishable in colour, then both or neither are red; yet clearly there must come a time when neither of the visible areas is red. This looks like a contradiction: on the one hand, no two adjacent areas differ in colour and the first is certainly red; on the other hand, the first area differs in colour from some subsequent colour.[2]

What do these paradoxical arguments have in common? In each case, the key word is *vague:* "tall", "heap", "red". A vague word admits of borderline cases, cases in which we don't know whether to apply the word or not, even though we have all the kinds of information which we would normally regard as sufficient to settle the matter. We may see how tall a man is, or even know his height to a millimetre, yet we may be unable to decide whether he counts as tall or not. We may see a collection of grains of sand, and even know exactly how many grains the collection contains, yet not know whether it should be called a heap or not. We may see a colour under the most favourable conditions imaginable, yet not know whether it should be called red or orange. This ignorance is not a manifestation of any failure to understand our language.

One common view, the predominant view until quite recently, is that this ignorance is explained by there being nothing to know. In borderline cases, there is simply no fact of the matter: no fact of the matter whether the man is tall or not, the collection a heap or not, the colour red or not. So prevalent has this view been that it has been common to *define* an object as a borderline case for a vague word as one for which there is no fact of the matter whether the word applies.[3] On this view, words like "tall", "heap" and "red" are seen as introducing no sharp boundary between things to which

2   How would one construct a parallel argument with the paradoxical conclusion that no men are bald?

3   Another common definition is: a borderline object for a word is one of which the word is neither definitely true nor definitely false. Does this amount to the same as the definition in terms of there being no fact of the matter?

they apply and things to which they do not. If we arrange people in a series, each a little shorter than the last, there is no such person as the last in the series to which the word "tall" truly applies, and no such person as the first in the series of which the word is false. On this view, vagueness is a semantic phenomenon. A semantic property, like that of being true, relates words to the world. The semantic view of vagueness sees it as a *special* way in which words may be related to the world, one according to which there is sometimes no fact of the matter whether the words apply to the world or not. (It is another question whether this property needs further to be explained in terms of some special feature of the world: see below, section 2.7.)[4]

Recently, an alternative view has resurfaced: vagueness is nothing more than a special kind of ignorance. On this view, the "epistemic" theory, there is a fact of the matter even in borderline cases, though a fact which we can never know. Vague words do introduce sharp boundaries, so (for example) there is a last tall man in a series of men of diminishing height, though we cannot tell which he is. I describe this view in more detail below (section 2.4).

Whether we adopt the epistemic view, upon which there is nothing more to vagueness than ignorance, or the more classical semantic view upon which vagueness also involves an absence of sharp boundaries, vagueness needs to be distinguished from relativity and from ambiguity; and it must be recognised as extremely widespread.

Consider the property of *being above average in height*. Assuming that there is no problem about assigning numbers to people as measures of their height, this is not a vague property. A person is above average in height just on condition that the number that measures his or her height is greater than the number that measures the average height, and this is a completely precise condition. However, being greater than the average height, though precise, is *relative* to a given population. Being above average in height for a Swede involves being taller than does being above average in height for an Eskimo, since the average height of Swedes is greater than the average height of Eskimos.

---

4 How could one who holds that vagueness is not a feature of reality (but only of our descriptions of reality) respond to the following argument?
   Mountains are part of reality, but they are vague. They have no sharp boundaries: it is vague where the mountain ends and the plain begins. So it is easy to see that vagueness is a feature of reality, and not just of our thought and talk.

As the example shows, relativity does not entail vagueness, since it can hold of precise expressions, like "is above average in height". Many vague predicates are also relative, but their relativity must not be confused with their vagueness. For example, "tall", unlike "above average in height", is vague and also relative. You can see that the vagueness does not entail the relativity by seeing that you could eliminate the relativity but leave the vagueness. If instead of "tall" we were to say "tall for a Swede", we would have eliminated some relativity, but the vagueness would remain.[5] We believe that the difference of 0.1" cannot make the difference between being tall for a Swede and not. This means that the argument of the opening paragraph will work as well for "tall for a Swede" as it did for "tall".[6]

Vagueness must also be distinguished from *ambiguity*. Consider the word "bank". It can mean the edge of a river or a financial institution. As a result, we do not know how to answer the question "Did he go to the bank this morning?". So far, there is a parallel with vagueness. We do not know how to answer the question "Is he bald?" if the person in question is a borderline case. However, there is a difference. In the case of ambiguity, a single sentence can be used to say, or ask, more than one thing. Before communication can proceed, the audience needs to determine *which* thing is being said or asked. In the bank example, there is no one answer because there is no one question. With vagueness it is different. If someone asks of a borderline case "Is he a child?", it is not that our problem in answering is the problem of knowing *which* question has been asked; there is only one possible question involved here. The problem is quite different: if the person of whom the question is asked is a borderline case, neither "Yes" nor "No" is a clearly correct answer. This question has a single vague meaning, and that is quite different from having two or more meanings.

Vagueness is a widespread feature of our thought. Consider the following list: "child", "book", "toy", "happy", "clever", "few", "cloudy", "pearl", "moustache", "game", "husband", "table".[7] Is this feature ineradicable? Could we replace our vague expressions by precise ones? We will answer this question differently, indeed understand it differently, depending as we incline to the epistemic

---

[5] Does the restriction to Swedes eliminate all relativity?
[6] Is "heap" relative in the way that "tall" is?
[7] Show that each of the words in the list is vague by briefly sketching a borderline case. Can you think of any words that are not vague?

view of vagueness (it is nothing but ignorance) or the semantic view (it involves a special word–world relation).

Consider the following argument. It is important to the role of the concept of childhood in our lives that the word "child" be vague. For example, we take ourselves to have special duties to children that we do not have to adults, but these duties are not relinquished overnight; they gradually fade away, just as childhood itself does. There is no sharp boundary to the end of our duties, just as there is no sharp boundary to the end of childhood. If we were to replace "child" by some more precise term, say "minor", as we have to for certain legal purposes, it would no longer be possible to express the obligations we feel. Our duties to people as children may end before or persist after their legal majority, depending on what age the law selects for coming of age, and depending on whether they are, as we say, "old for their age" or "young for their age".

Consider a second example of the same general kind of argument. It is important to the role of the concept of redness in our lives that the word "red" be vague. In particular, the vagueness is essential to the observational character of "red", to the fact that we can under favourable conditions tell just by looking whether something is red or not. If we replaced "red" by an expression having sharp boundaries, say one defined in terms of wavelengths, then the right way to approach applying it would be by an exact determination of the wavelength: in losing the vagueness, we lose the observational character.

These arguments are unsatisfactory twice over. Firstly, they seem simply to presuppose a semantic rather than an epistemic conception of vagueness, without supplying a justification. Secondly, they are fallacious. The uncontroversial premises in the case of "red" are these:

(1)   Under some conditions, and for some objects, we can confidently apply or deny "red" simply on the basis of observation.

(2)   For some objects, we cannot confidently either apply or deny "red".

These properties could hold of an expression which draws sharp boundaries, for example "is more than 6' tall". Under some conditions, and for some objects, we could be confident, on the basis of observation alone, whether to apply or deny the predicate. This is consistent with the fact that, at least unless we have a ruler, there will be objects about which we are in doubt: those close in height to 6'. The argument erred in supposing that if a colour word were defined in terms of exact wavelengths, we would have to use an exact wavelength-measurer to apply it. The argument failed to show that an absence of sharp boundaries was required for, or helped explain, the observational character of some vague expressions.[8]

The argument about childhood is also defective. To say that we have special duties of care to children is not in itself to say that there is a proportion between how demanding the duties are and how old a person is. If we do need to say the latter, then we seem to be able to say it straightforwardly, as I have just done, and in a way which does not require "child" to fail to have sharp boundaries. One can also accept that childhood fades gradually away without accepting that "child" draws no sharp boundaries. To show this by analogy: if one is under 21, the time remaining until the moment of one's twenty-first birthday gradually diminishes, but not in a way that requires lack of sharp boundaries.

Whatever the explanation, there can be no doubt that vagueness is a very widespread phenomenon. Hence there are plenty of opportunities for constructing paradoxical sorites arguments. We must look at these more closely, and see what responses are possible.

2.2   Sorites paradoxes: the options

In this section, I will make more explicit one form of soritical reasoning, and at the end of it will lay out some possible kinds of response.

Sorites reasoning depends upon the supposition that vague expressions are "tolerant": small changes don't affect the applicability of the word. If someone is tall, so is a person a millimetre shorter; if a collection is a heap, so is one otherwise similar but with just one grain less. The paradox arises because big changes, ones which obviously do affect whether or not the word applies, can be constructed out of small changes.

Let us set out one version of a sorites argument in a more explicit form, in which we can clearly identify the impact of the supposed tolerance of vague words. The first premise might be:

8   Assess whether the following consideration might help reinstate an interesting connection between vagueness and observationality:
In the case of "is more than 6' tall" one could in principle decide all cases, if one had the help of a ruler. By contrast, in the case of "red", nothing could help one decide borderline cases.

(1)   A 10,000-grained collection is a heap.

The second premise, instancing the supposed tolerance of "heap", might be as follows:

(2)   If a 10,000-grained collection is a heap, then so is a 9,999-grained collection.

Tolerance underwrites numerous further premises of this form, for example:

(3)   If a 9,999-grained collection is a heap, then so is a 9,998-grained collection.

And so on. Let us call the first premise the *categorical* premise and the others the *conditional* premises. (A conditional statement is one of the form "If ..., then ...".)

We are just as inclined to hold to these conditional premises when they concern small numbers as when they concern large numbers, and just as inclined to hold to them for cases in which there is genuine doubt about whether a collection is heap-sized as when there is no such doubt. For example:

(10,000) If a 2-grained collection is a heap, so is a 1-grained collection.

We are firmly convinced that neither a 1-grained nor a 2-grained collection is a heap; but this does not stop us holding that *if* a 2-grained collection is a heap, then so is a 1-grained collection. We are reflecting our conviction that taking away a grain cannot turn something from a heap into a non-heap. The conviction also attaches to borderline cases, for example:

(9,925) If a 77-grained collection is a heap, so is a 76-grained collection.

Here we may be in genuine doubt about whether either collection deserves to be called a heap. Yet the conditional reflects our confidence that both or neither are heaps, and this is simply another way of putting the tolerance principle: a difference of a grain cannot be the difference between a heap and a non-heap.

We do not yet have a paradox. To get it, we apply to these premises a general principle of reasoning: given p, and a conditional of the form "if p, then q", we can derive q. This principle is still called by the Latin name it was given in the middle ages: *modus ponendo ponens*, or *modus ponens*, for short. Applying it to our first and second premises yields:

A 9,999-grained collection is a heap.

Applying the principle again to the above and premise (3) yields:

A 9,998-grained collection is a heap.

Continuing in the same way, we finally end up with the result that a 1-grained (or, for that matter, even a 0-grained) collection is a heap, and this is the absurdity.

As with any paradox there are three possible responses to consider:

(a)   Accept the conclusion of the argument.
(b)   Reject the reasoning as faulty.
(c)   Reject one or more premises.

For some vague words, (a) may seem a totally unpromising possibility to explore. Could anything reconcile us to the suggestion that everyone is tall, or that a heap cannot be demolished grain by grain so that no heap is left, or that all colours are red? Some philosophers have used sorites reasoning to argue for conclusions of just this kind. I give one example in the next section.

2.3   Accepting the conclusion: Unger's view

Consider the following argument:

(1)   Given just one gramme of wood, you cannot make a table.
(2)   If you cannot make a table out of n grammes of wood, then you cannot make a table out of $n+1$ grammes.
(3)   Hence you cannot make a table, no matter how many grammes of wood you have.

Crucial to the argument is the idea that a gramme cannot make the difference between not enough wood to make a table and enough wood. (If you feel doubts about this, try reducing the amount to a millionth of a gramme.)

There is a close analogy between this reasoning and the reasoning of the previous section concerning heaps. That reasoning seemed to establish that heaps are indestructible: however many grains you take away from a heap, it remains a heap. The present reasoning runs in the reverse order, and seems to establish that tables are uncreatable: however many bits you add, you still don't have a table. This conclusion amounts to the claim that there are no tables.

Nothing essentially depends upon the notion of literally "making" a table. We could use similar reasoning to show that there are no stones. If a region contains only one gramme of solid material, it does not contain a stone. If a region contains n grammes of solid material but not a stone, then a region as similar as possible except that it contains $n+1$ grammes of solid material also does not contain a stone. If we start with a region which we take, intuitively, to be occupied by a stone, and focus on a one gramme part of it, and then successively expand our considerations outwards by including, one at a time, a further adjacent region occupied by a gramme of matter, we appear to be able to conclude, contrary to the original intuition, that however far we expand we will not get to a region containing a stone. Generalizing, the conclusion amounts to the claim that there are no stones.

These conclusions seem strange, but they have been advanced with at least apparent seriousness by Unger (1979a). We can make them seem less mad by putting them in a certain perspective. Perhaps the conclusion we should draw from the existence of the sorites paradoxes is that vague concepts are deeply flawed: they commit us to absurdities. A flawed concept is one under which nothing can fall. So even though the world may contain all sorts of stuff, it is wrong to say that we can divide it up using concepts flawed by vagueness. Rather, we have to say that nothing matches these concepts: there are no tables, no stones, etc.[9]

One cannot dismiss this point of view as mad. However, it would not be wrong to regard it as something of a last resort, and Unger himself accepts that if there were some way of defusing sorites paradoxes, his own solution would be unattractive. So we need to look at alternative responses.

Sorites reasoning appears to be extremely simple and to use only the fundamental logical principle of modus ponens, so the prospect of rejecting it as invalid (response (b) above) is not initially tempting.

The most obvious response to explore is (c): reject one or more premises. The next two sections explore two ways in which this might be motivated.

---

[9]* How should someone who adopts Unger's viewpoint respond to the argument which concludes that even a 1-grained collection would make a heap?

2.4   Rejecting the premises: the epistemic theory

The epistemic theory of vagueness holds that vagueness is nothing but ignorance. So far as their semantics go, vague words are just like precise ones: they draw sharp boundaries. The epistemic theorist will see sorites paradoxical arguments as proving his view. When the arguments take the form displayed in the previous section, the epistemic theorist sees them as establishing by *reductio ad absurdum* the falsity of at least one premise. (An argument by *reductio ad absurdum* is one which starts by deducing an absurdity from some premises, in order to demonstrate that one of the premises must be false.) Since, on the epistemic view, there is a sharp line dividing heaps from non-heaps, there is a least number, n, such that an n-grained collection is a heap, so it must be false that:

> if an n-grained collection is a heap, then so is an $n–1$-grained collection.

The epistemic theory is generally greeted with incredulity. How could there be a sharp boundary to the heaps, the bald men, the tall men, childhood, and so on? For, it may be suggested, if there really were such boundaries we ought, at least in principle, to be able to discover where they lie, whereas it is plainly impossible that we should do this.

The epistemic theorist has two things to say in response. First, he will insist that he does not accept the *verificationist theory of meaning*, or *verificationism* for short. This theory, characteristic of the logical positivism which flourished in the middle years of the twentieth century, has it that any sentence we can understand is one which, in principle, we could tell to be true, or false, as the case may be. Verificationism is inconsistent with the epistemic theory, which holds that if an object is a borderline case for a vague word, we have no means of determining the truth or falsehood of an application of the word to the object. However, at least in the crude form presented here, verificationism is now not widely accepted, so few would wish to attack the epistemic theory from this angle.

The epistemic theorist's second response is to explain why we are incurably ignorant in borderline cases. It springs, on his view, from the fact that our cognitive mechanisms, for example our senses, require a margin of error. Suppose that a certain patch p is the last red patch on the wall we described earlier, where red shades gradually give way to less and less red ones, and finally to orange ones, and so on. Suppose, moreover, that we *believe* that p is the last red patch in the series. The epistemic theorist argues that

[handwritten margin note: vagueness depends on "n" being a precise number which divides whether a property is existent or not.]

this belief cannot count as knowledge, for there must have been an element of luck in our coming to have this true belief. This is because we cannot reliably distinguish *p* from its neighbours: from a patch to the right which is not red, or from a patch to the left which, though red, is not the last red in the series. Knowledge requires being non-accidentally right. The fact that there is a margin of error in our perceptual system means that we could never have knowledge of which the last patch is.

The epistemic theorist may thus explain our ignorance, but he still has to establish the claim that there is anything to be ignorant of: he still has to establish that vague predicates draw sharp boundaries. Taking up this challenge in full would involve showing that alternative responses to sorites paradoxes are inadequate.[10]

2.5   Rejecting the premises: supervaluations

One can reject one of the conditional premises without adopting the epistemic theory. One way is the *theory of supervaluations*. I will state this theory, and then go on to indicate some problems for it.

Let us say that an object falls within the *positive extension* of a predicate, say "heap", just on condition that the object definitely possesses the relevant property (say, is definitely a heap); that it falls within the *negative extension* just on condition that it definitely lacks the property; and that otherwise it falls within the *penumbra*. On the semantic conception of vagueness, a vague word is one for which some objects do, or could, fall within its penumbra. Using this terminology, let us consider one line of thought designed to explain why the premises of the paradoxical argument strike us as true, while not really being so.

A vague expression can be thought of as giving us some leeway with respect to the objects in its penumbra. One is at liberty to place these objects in either the positive or negative extension, though one is not required to place them in either. We tend to exercise this licence in the way shown by the tolerance principle; that is, we tend to think that if we have exercised it in one way with respect to an

---

10 Evaluate the following argument against the epistemic theory, as applied to colour predicates:

If a predicate stands for a manifest property (one which under some conditions detectably obtains), then under optimal conditions for manifestation, if there is a fact of the matter whether or not it obtains, that fact is detectable. We can view a region of the coloured wall (one borderline for "red") under optimal conditions without being able to detect the presence or absence of redness; so there is no fact concerning whether that region is or is not red.

[margin note: penumbra — could or could not be possessed of a certain property.]

object, we must exercise it in the same way with respect to a closely similar one. However, this is not obligatory. If there is no question of a vague word being really true or really false of an object in its penumbra, we are at liberty to decide the matter either way. In particular, there would be nothing wrong with placing a 5' 10" man in the positive extension of "tall" and a man shorter than this by 0.1" in the negative extension. There is nothing that requires us to make any such choice; but equally there is nothing to rule it out. We are not in the realm of *how things are with the object*; rather, we are in the realm of *how we choose to speak of the objects*. Once we accept this, so the line of thought goes, we see that the tolerance principle should not be adhered to, or at least should not be adhered to with respect to penumbral cases.

To reformulate the suggestion (I will keep to the "heap" example, but the suggestion is meant to apply generally): one speaks *truly* in applying "heap" to an object just on condition that the object is definitely a heap, that is, falls within the positive extension; one speaks *falsely* just on condition that the object is definitely not a heap, that is, falls within the negative extension. If one applies "heap" to an object in the penumbra of the word, one speaks neither truly nor falsely. The idea is to go on from this to show that the premises of the paradox are not all true.

The categorical premise does not apply to a penumbral object, and thus the present suggestion, quite rightly, leaves its truth untouched. So which premise is not true? It must be one (or more) of the conditional ones, and presumably one about objects that are penumbral for "heap": collections (we are pretending) with seventy or so members. Nothing that has so far been said entails anything about what it is, on the supervaluational account, for conditionals to be true, or false, or neither true nor false.

Suppose α and β are in the penumbra of "heap", and that α has one more grain than β. On the basis of what has been said so far, "α is a heap" is neither true nor false; likewise "β is a heap". However, what has so far been suggested does not speak to the question of whether or not the following conditional is true:

If α is a heap, then β is a heap.

If the supervaluational account is to release us from the paradox, it must explain how it comes about that some such premise is not true.

The needed refinement can be attained like this. Any choice of where to draw a sharp line between heaps and non-heaps within the penumbra is acceptable; as we can put it, any *sharpening* of

Heap is only true after you chose a sharpening to define a heap & draw the line.

"heap" which draws a line in the penumbra is acceptable. We ascribe "heap" truly just when what we say would have been true however one might have drawn the line, that is, whatever sharpening we had chosen; and we ascribe it falsely just when what we say would have been false whatever sharpening we had chosen. Applying this idea in general, we can say that a sentence is true iff it is true with respect to every sharpening, false iff it is false with respect to every sharpening, and otherwise is neither true nor false. ("Iff" abbreviates "if and only if".) Since ascribing "heap" to something in the penumbra will be true relative to some sharpenings and false relative to others, the ascription meets neither the condition for being true, nor that for being false: it is, as we wanted, neither true nor false.

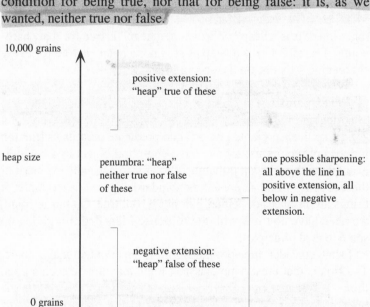

Figure 2.1: One possible sharpening of the word "heap".

Suppose as before that α and β are in the penumbra of "heap". In particular, suppose that α is a 76-grained collection and that β is a 75-grained collection. Is the following sentence true for every sharpening?

If α is a heap, so is β.

No. For consider the sharpening, σ, which assigns all 76-grained and larger collections to the positive extension of "heap", and all smaller collections to its negative extension. "α is a heap" is true relative to σ, but "β is a heap" is false relative to σ. A sentence of *[handwritten margin note: since the sharpening was not part of the conditional, it can be changed to show (11).]*

the form "if ..., then ..." cannot be true if the first clause – the antecedent – is true and the second – the consequent – is false. Thus the conditional is not true for σ and so is not true relative to all sharpenings; therefore, the conditional is not true. Neither is it false, as analogous reasoning would show.[11]

It is not that, on this account, *any* sentence in which a vague word is applied to an object in its penumbra is neither true nor false. For example, the sentence

(S)   α is either a heap or not a heap

is true with respect to all sharpenings, and so true. A sharpening draws the line somewhere. Wherever it draws it, α will either fall in the positive or the negative extension. Hence, for any sharpening, either "α is a heap" or "α is not a heap" is true for that sharpening. Therefore "α is a heap or α is not a heap" is true for every sharpening – that is, on the account, *true*.[12]

To sum up, the supervaluational account purports to dissolve the paradox by showing that not all the premises of the paradoxical argument are true. In particular, the principle of tolerance does not hold. The licence granted by a vague predicate permits us (though it does not require us) to take any penumbral object as a counter-example to the relevant principle of tolerance. One alleged merit of the account is that it preserves standard logic. For example, it brings all instances of "either *p* or not *p*" out true. On this account, we need have no truck with the response I labelled (b): giving up some logical principles.

I shall consider three problems for the supervaluational account. The first is that preserving classical logic may not be such a good thing. Vagueness has often been supposed to throw doubt on the logical principle called the Law of Excluded Middle, exemplified by:

Either he is an adult or he is not.

It might be suggested that given that there are borderline cases of adults, we should be reluctant to affirm this instance of the Law. For consider how affirming it might be exploited in an argument which could, not unreasonably, be held to be flawed:

---

11   How could it be shown that the conditional is not false?
12   Does the supervaluational account entail the following:
       "α is a heap" is true or "α is not a heap" is true?
    What interesting point about the supervaluational treatment of "or" does your answer highlight?

Either he is an adult or he is not. If he is an adult, then watching the hard-porn movie will do him no harm. If he is not an adult, then he will not understand it, so, in this case too, watching it will do him no harm. Either way, it will do him no harm to watch it.

We might object: the argument fails to take account of the person on the borderline between childhood and adulthood. For him, it is not right to say "Either he is an adult or he is not". It is precisely because he is between childhood and adulthood that seeing the movie might harm him.

The second problem for the supervaluational theory is that it assigns intuitively the wrong truth value to a sentence which is central to sorites paradoxes:

> For some number n, an n-grained collection is a heap but an $(n-1)$-grained collection is not.

We intuitively tend to believe that this sentence is false (and likewise similar sentences for other vague words).[13] Indeed, that it is false is, for the semantic theorist, a definitional consequence of the vagueness of the predicate: vagueness is a matter of there being no sharp boundary. However, on the supervaluational theory the sentence comes out as true, since it is true with respect to every sharpening.[14] This is unacceptable.

The third problem for the supervaluational theory is that it works with an inadequate conception of vagueness. One inadequacy is that it assumes a characterization of vagueness which is insufficient. It assumes that a vague word can be associated with three sets: its positive extension, its penumbra and its negative extension. However, predicates which, intuitively, are not vague may also be associated with three such sets. We might define a minor by the following clauses:

(1)   People who have not reached their 17th birthday are minors.

(2)   People who have reached their 18th birthday are not minors.

Then "minor" will be associated with three sets: its positive extension, fixed by clause (1); its negative extension, fixed by clause (2); and its "penumbra", fixed as what remains, that is, 17-year-olds. Yet intuitively "minor", thus defined, is not vague.

---

13   Would the epistemic theorist agree with this judgement?
14   How is this demonstrated? (Cf. Sanford 1976.)

We might justify this intuition by saying that the clauses which define "minor" are entirely precise. What leads to three sets is not lack of precision, but lack of *completeness*. Arguably, we can find the same phenomenon among familiar words. Thus perhaps "pearl" has as its positive extension anything made of the correct material and formed in an oyster; as its negative extension anything not of the right material; and as its penumbra pearl-sized lumps of pearl-material synthesized outside of any oyster. I suggest we should see "pearl" not as vague, but as incomplete: there is a blank where there should be a rule.

The problem I am posing for the supervaluational theory is that it cannot distinguish between vagueness and incompleteness, for it will offer the same treatment for any predicate which can be associated with three sets as positive extension, negative extension and penumbra. The difference between incompleteness and vagueness is controversial. I claim that the meaning of an incomplete word like "pearl" does not speak to pearl-sized lumps of pearl-material. By contrast, I claim that the meaning of vague words like "heap" does say something about penumbral cases. It says that as a competent user you must recognize borderline cases as borderline, and hence should not confidently and without a sense of stipulation apply or deny the predicate; and that your use remains governed by such principles as: if α is borderline for "heap" and β is otherwise similar except that it has fewer grains, β is not a clear case of a heap.

The other aspect of the alleged inadequacy of the supervaluational theorist's account of vagueness is that it fails to allow for "higher order vagueness". The account presupposes that there is a sharp line between the positive extension of a vague predicate and its penumbra; and a further sharp line between the penumbra and the negative extension. This presupposition, which emerges in the definition of a sharpening, does not do justice to our intuitive conceptions, according to which we recognize higher order vagueness: that there is as much vagueness about where the penumbral cases of "heap" begin as there is about where the clear cases of non-heaps begin. In other words, we tend to believe that vagueness as much affects the supposed boundary between positive extension and penumbra as it does the supposed boundary between positive extension and negative extension. We intuitively contrast *clear* borderline cases and others. For example, one might think that a sixteen-year-old is a clear borderline case with respect to "child", whereas one might be unsure whether a fifteen-year-old is a borderline case with respect to "child". Perhaps we should classify fifteen-year-olds as children; or perhaps we should classify them as borderline cases of children. Here we seem to face just the kind of doubts that we have concerning whether to classify someone as a child or as an adult.

To make the point another way, we could devise a new version of the paradox, like the old except that "is a heap" or "is a child" is replaced by "is definitely a heap" or "is definitely a child", where we think of borderline cases as those to which the word can neither definitely be applied nor definitely denied.[15] This shows that "is definitely a heap" and "is definitely a child" are vague, and hence that it is vague where the positive extensions of "heap" and "child" end and their penumbras begin.

If there were no higher order vagueness, there should be no difficulty in principle about dividing the extension of a vague predicate into three quite precise sets: the things falling into its positive extension, the things falling into its negative extension, and the things falling into its penumbra. (If what was said earlier was right, this way of thinking would not enable us to distinguish between vagueness and incompleteness; but that is a distinct problem.) If a predicate exhibits higher order vagueness, we could not effect such a tripartite division. In that case, the notion of a sharpening would itself be vague: some division of objects into a positive and a negative extension would be borderline for "sharpening", perhaps one which assigned fifteen-year-olds to a positive extension with respect to "child".

It may be that a version of supervaluational theory could be developed which would allow for higher order vagueness, by allowing that "sharpening" is vague. There is no threat in this to the theory's power to block the sorites paradox, since that block depends upon there being at least one clear case of a sharpening which will make at least one conditional premise untrue.[16] But the development of such a theory brings its own difficulties; and the development would not of itself make the other problems for a supervaluational theory go away.[17]

---

[15] Write out the categorical premise of a paradoxical argument of this kind, and give one example of the conditional premises. What is the unacceptable apparent consequence of these premises?

[16] This assumes that, even if "sharpening" is vague, each vague predicate has at least one clear case of a sharpening. What example could you give to illustrate this?

[17] How would you assess the following objection to a version of the supervaluational account which allows that the notion of a sharpening is vague?

2.6   Rejecting the reasoning: degrees of truth

Let us take stock. We envisaged three possible responses to the paradox:

(a)   to accept the conclusion;
(b)   to reject the reasoning; or
(c)   to reject one or more premises.

We have taken (a) to be a last resort. We have explored two versions of response (c): the epistemic theory and the supervaluational theory. I now want to turn to what has often been classified as a (b)-type response. (As we will see, this classification is open to question.)

We are strongly disinclined to allow that there could be anything wrong with modus ponens. Nevertheless, some theorists have tried to place the blame on this principle of reasoning, and I will try to explain their grounds.

When asked to assess a claim to the effect that a sixteen-year-old is an adult, it is natural to say something like "That's *to some extent* true", or "There's *a certain amount of truth* in that"; likewise whenever a vague predicate is applied to a borderline case. The response to the paradoxical argument I now wish to consider takes this very seriously. The suggestion is that we introduce *degrees of truth*. That a predicate like "adult" definitely applies to an object will be registered by the maximum degree of truth, conventionally 1. That a predicate definitely does not apply to an object will be registered by the minimum degree of truth, conventionally 0. Borderline cases will be registered by an intermediate degree of truth. Ascribing "bald" to a man who nearly qualifies as bald will rate a degree of truth closer to 1 than applying it to a man who nearly qualifies as non-bald. A degree of truth theory thus takes very seriously the point that the meaning of a vague word says something about the borderline cases. The theory seeks to represent *what* the meaning says by the various degrees of truth.

How can a degree theory dissolve the paradoxical argument? It must assign the highest degree of truth to the categorical premise of the argument and the lowest degree to the conclusion; how will it treat the conditional premises?

If "sharpening" is vague, then no sentence can be definitely true. Truth involves appeal to *all* sharpenings; what is to count as a sharpening is vague, so it is not definitely true of any collection that these are all the sharpenings there are (with respect to a given predicate). However, it is absurd to suggest that "Yul Brynner was bald" is anything other than *definitely* true.

Suppose collections of grains of sand start becoming penumbral for "heap" at around the 100 mark. Consider the following conditional:

If this 95-grained collection is a heap, so is this 94-grained collection.

What should the degree theorist say? The antecedent of the conditional is

This 95-grained collection is a heap.

The consequent is

This 94-grained collection is a heap.

According to the degree theory, the antecedent is nearly but not quite true. Perhaps it is assigned the degree of truth 0.96. The consequent is also nearly true, but not quite so nearly true as the antecedent. Perhaps it is assigned the degree of truth 0.95. What degree of truth should be assigned to the conditional itself?

There is room for variation in detail, but the general idea is that if the antecedent of a conditional is truer than its consequent, then the conditional cannot be wholly true; thus the conditional in question needs to be assigned a degree of truth less than 1. The justification for this lies in part with the analogy with the standard case in which degrees of truth are not taken into account: we say that a conditional whose antecedent is true and whose consequent is false cannot be true, because a conditional should not lead from truth to falsehood. Analogously, a conditional should not lead to a lower degree of truth. The greater the amount of truth lost in the passage from antecedent to consequent, the lower the degree of truth assignable to the whole conditional.

So far, the degree theorist's response is of type (c): reject the premises. On this theory the conditional premises, though very nearly true, are not quite true. Hence we need not be fully committed to them. Hence the paradoxical argument does not commit us to the paradoxical conclusion. However, the account needs to go further. Even if we are not fully committed to the premises, they are very nearly true. The degree theorist has to explain how we can have premises that are all very nearly true, yet a conclusion that is wholly false.

One way to do this, though not the only one, is to deny that the conclusion follows from the premises, and thus deny the validity of modus ponens; this is a response of type (b). On the degree-theoretic account envisaged here, modus ponens does not preserve degree of truth: the conclusion of an argument of the form "If p, then q; p, therefore q" may have a lower degree of truth than any of the premises. The conditional mentioned earlier, about 95- and 94-grained collections, is extremely close to the whole truth; perhaps it has a truth degree of 0.99. The antecedent, we suggested, had truth degree 0.96. Yet applying modus ponens yields a conclusion with truth degree only 0.95, lower than the truth degree of either of the premises. Modus ponens is valid as applied to sentences with the extreme truth degrees, 0 or 1: that is, one cannot get a conclusion with degree less than 1 from premises of degree 1. However, in the intermediate degrees the application of modus ponens can lead to a "leakage" of truth. The leakage may be small for each application, but can be large if the number of applications is large, as in the case of the paradoxical argument; and it can be regarded as a sufficient condition for the invalidity of modus ponens.

We earlier thought that modus ponens was a principle that simply could not be abandoned. What the degree theorist suggests, however, may well be consistent with all we really believed about modus ponens. There are two reasons for this.

The first is that normally we have in mind only the cases in which modus ponens is applied to sentences that are (*completely*) true or (*completely*) false. For these cases, the degree theorist's view agrees with our intuitions.

The second is that it is arguably not correct to assume, as we have so far, that an argument's validity is properly understood in terms of preservation of degree of truth, in the sense that the conclusion of a valid argument must have a degree of truth no lower than that of the least true premise. Perhaps it is better (and it would certainly preserve tempting analogies with degrees of belief) to say that the conclusion of a valid argument cannot have a greater degree of falsehood than the sum of the degrees of falsehood of its premises (Edgington 1992). (If a number, n, measures a degree of truth, then $1-n$ measures a corresponding degree of falsehood.) Then degree theory need give us no reason to say that modus ponens is not valid.[18] If we adopt this position, we must reclassify the degree theory as one which rejects the premises of sorites arguments, or rather, does not fully accept them.

A full defence of the degree of truth theory would require the consideration of a number of issues that I shall briefly mention. First, it is necessary to say something about what a degree of truth is. Second, some account must be given of the source and justification of the numbers that are to be assigned as degrees. Third, the

---

[18] Why not?

[handwritten margin note: The degree theory is valid because it applies to only definitely true or false conclusions. Thus, the degree of falsehood is null and the degree of truth = the degree of truth of the premises.]

full implications of the degree theory for logic must be set out and defended.

A degree theory treats vagueness as a semantic matter, not as an epistemic one. The semantic theory of degrees of truth registers the semantics of a vague predicate as different in kind (since involving the intermediate degrees) from the semantics of a precise predicate. So the first thing a degree theorist would have to do is refute the epistemic theory. Let us suppose that this has somehow been accomplished. The remainder of the defence presupposes that vagueness involves there being no sharp boundaries.

A key property of truth is marked by the platitude that we aim to believe what is true. If we could show that degrees of truth had an analogous property, we would have gone some way toward explaining what a degree of truth is.

Suppose that you are fairly sure that Arkle won the Gold Cup in 1960. Your memory may fail you about some matters, but you are pretty reliable about the history of the turf. You reckon that you have a very much better than fifty–fifty chance of being right that it was Arkle. If you are at all attracted by gambling, it will be rational for you to bet on his having won, if you can get odds as good as even; for if you follow this policy generally, you will win more than fifty times out of a hundred. A policy that will result in your winning more than you lose is a policy that it is rational for you to pursue. It is rational to perform a particular action that is required by the pursuit of a rational policy.

We want to believe what is true, but we do not always know what is true. The greater the confidence we have in a proposition, the more it affects us as if we believed it to be true. If we are almost certain that our house will not burn down, we will not spend much money insuring it against fire. If we are almost certain that we shall be alive tomorrow, we do not waste much time today making arrangements for our death.

It is rational, then, for our beliefs to vary in strength, reflecting variations in our confidence, and thus variations in our assessment of the quality of our information. We may be less than totally confident because we are less than fully informed. Here, the less than total confidence mirrors our deficiencies.

Vagueness may also lead to less than total confidence. Suppose you know, having had it on impeccable authority, that all and only red mushrooms are poisonous. You wish to kill Jones. All other things being equal, you would prefer to poison him, and you would prefer to do so using mushrooms, so that it will look like an accident. However, the only mushroom you can find right now, though reddish, is not a clear case of red. Will you use it to try to poison Jones? It depends upon how important it is to you to succeed, how important it is to succeed at first attempt, and how soon Jones must die if his death is to be of service to you. How reasonable it is to use the mushroom depends upon the weights you assign to these other factors, and upon your degree of confidence in the redness of the mushroom. The more confident you are that this mushroom is really red, the more reasonable it is to use it; the less confident, the less reasonable. In the context, this confidence affects your action in the same way as would a lack of confidence springing from lack of information, from fear that your memory fails you, or whatever. From the point of view of action, it is rather as if you had less than total confidence in the statement "This mushroom will do the job".

However, there is also a sharp contrast. Less than total confidence springing from incomplete evidence or fear of unreliability mirrors our deficiencies; less than complete confidence springing from an appreciation of vagueness arguably does not. If the mushroom is a borderline case, it is not your fault that you are unsure whether it should be counted as red; indeed, you would be at fault if you took yourself to be required firmly to classify it either as red or as not red. Continuing our assumption that the epistemic theory has been rejected, we can go further: no matter how perfect your memory and senses, no matter how infallible your reasoning, the mushroom stays on the borderline. On the question of whether the mushroom is red, an omniscient being could do no better.

Where we have incomplete information, or unreliability, there is a chance of improvement: we can in theory raise our confidence by getting more information. Where we have vagueness, there may be no chance of improvement. Given your language and the way the world is, you can do no better than have partial confidence in "This mushroom is red". Truth is what we seek in belief. It is that than which we cannot do better. So where partial confidence is the best that is even theoretically available, we need a corresponding concept of partial truth or degree of truth. Where vagueness is at issue, we must aim at a degree of belief that matches the degree of truth, just as, where there is no vagueness, we must aim to believe just what is true.

The second part of a defence of a degree of truth theory is to explain and justify the origin of the numbers that are assigned as degrees of truth. Suppose there are two mushrooms, both borderline cases of red, but one redder than the other. If you want to commit the poisoning, and you have full confidence in the information that all and only red ones kill, you should choose the redder if you choose either. The redder one must be closer to being a definite case of red. This suggests how we could justify assigning degrees of truth: we have to assign a higher degree to a redder object; or, if we are dealing with "heap", we must assign a higher degree to penumbral collections the more numerous they are. In short, the source and justification of assignments of degrees of truth would lie in our comparative judgements involving penumbral cases.[19,20]

The third part of the defence of a degree theory would involve justifying how one ascribes degrees of truth to logically complex sentences. Degree theories of the kind under consideration, in which the degree of truth of a complex sentence is determined by the degree of truth of its constituents, depart from ordinary, so-called classical, logic. Whereas classical logic has it that all sentences of the form "p and not-p" are false, and all sentences of the form "p or not-p" are true, some degree theorists demur. On their view, when p has only a medium degree of truth, "p and not-p" will not be completely false, and "p or not-p" will not be completely true. We have already seen, in the case of the argument about the harmful effects of watching hard-porn movies, that there is at least some case for holding that, if p is vague, "p or not-p" is not without qualification true. Furthermore, the naturalness of "It is and it isn't", as a response to the question whether a borderline-case mushroom is red, gives at least a preliminary indication that the degree theorist is right to recognize that not all instances of "p and not-p" are completely false.

However, there are problems. Standard forms of degree theory assign a conjunction a degree of truth equal to that of the least true conjunct. This means that, if x is a clear case of something red, y is a borderline case of red, and both x and y are, to the same degree, intermediate cases of something small, the conjunctions "x is red and x is small" and "y is red and y is small" will be assigned the same intermediate degree of truth, which is unintuitive.[21] Again,

[handwritten margin note: if p is a borderline case or vague]

---

19 How would you respond to the following objection?
   It is one thing to say that the comparative form of "red", viz. "redder than", is to be used as the basis for assigning degrees in connection with "red"; but it is quite another thing to apply this to "heap". The basis for the assignments would be comparisons involving "heaper than"; but this is nonsense.

20 How would you respond to the following objection?
   I agree that there are degrees of redness, but I cannot see that this means that there are degrees of truth.

21 Which conjunction do you think should have the higher degree of truth? Cf. Edgington (1992).

suppose Eve is definitely female and a borderline case for being an adult, so that "Eve is an adult" is assigned an intermediate degree of truth. Assume that it is definitely true that a woman is an adult female. Standard degree theory cannot distinguish between "Eve is an adult or Eve is a woman" and "Eve is an adult and Eve is not a woman", assigning both the same intermediate degree (Fine 1975).

The degree theory, like the supervaluation theory, appears to be at risk from considerations relating to higher order vagueness. On the coloured wall discussed previously, red gradually gives way to orange from left to right. At the left end, a sentence "This patch is red" will presumably be assigned degree 1. However, which is the last patch relative to which the sentence is assigned degree 1? If we allow that there is a last such patch, then it seems that we have introduced a borderline after all: between the definite reds and the others. If we say that there is no such patch, we seem to be committed to the absurdity that even when the sentence is applied to an orange patch it is still awarded the maximum degree of truth.

Part of the problem here is that we tend to think of semantic theories, like supervaluational theory or degrees of truth theory, as themselves expressed in a sharp language (the metalanguage). This means that we tend to think that vagueness can be described in precise terms. The phenomenon of higher order vagueness suggests (though it does not entail) that we are mistaken in this tendency.

If we try to describe a vague language by a vague one, we may not have conquered the problems concerning vagueness with which we began. Sorites paradoxes may threaten the language in which our semantics is expressed. If "has degree of truth 1" is precise, then it seems to draw a sharp boundary where no boundary should be. If it is vague, we will be tempted to suppose that if applying "red" to one of two indistinguishable patches merits degree of truth 1, so does applying it to the other, and we will be set on the familiar slippery sorites slope.

I believe that there are two promising options. One is the epistemic theory: it sounds mad, but I know of no way of decisively refuting it. The other is a semantic theory couched in a vague language that is constructed in such a way as to be free from paradox (Tye 1994). The crucial idea has to be that for some sentences there is no fact of the matter concerning how they are treated in the semantics: the semantics does not entail that they are true, does not entail that they are false, does not entail that they are neither true nor false, and so on. There must also be no fact of the matter about just which these sentences are.

2.7   Vague objects?

Are there vague *objects,* or is vagueness something that arises, not from the way the world itself is, but rather from how we describe it? This question is answered by the epistemic theory: the home of vagueness lies in our cognitive faculties, not in the world. However, it is left open by the semantic approach. The general feature of this approach is that, for some words and some states of affairs, there is no definite fact of the matter whether the words apply or fail to apply to the states of affairs. One could explain this in terms of vagueness in the words; but one might alternatively think that the world could, or even must, contribute to the explanation.

We can start by reverting to an earlier question (see footnote 4). The argument for discussion went like this:

> Mountains are part of reality, but they are vague. They have no sharp boundaries: it is vague where the mountain ends and the plain begins. So it is easy to see that vagueness is a feature of reality, and not just of our thought and talk.

Even if we like the conclusion, we should not accept this argument for it. Given our language, which contains words like "mountain", we can ask a vague question: does this spot belong to the mountain or to the plain? However, if we could give a complete description of the world without making use of such a vague expression, we would have no inclination to infer from the vagueness of the question to the vagueness of the world. We would not seem to be greatly handicapped, in describing the world, if we lacked the word "mountain": we could just draw the contour lines on our maps. In many cases, for example "heap", our use of the vague word is guided by sharp underlying facts, for example, by (in part) how many grains the collection contains. Each collection has a definite number of members, and we could in principle give more information about a collection by the sharp fact of how many members it has than by the vague matter of whether or not it is a heap. So the displayed argument does not undermine the view that vagueness comes from our thought and talk, rather than being an objective feature of the world.

Let us consider an old story. Theseus had a ship. When a plank rotted, it was replaced. After a while, none of the original planks were left. Likewise for the other kinds of parts of the ship – masts, sails, and so forth. Did Theseus's ship survive? Suppose that someone had kept the rotted planks and other parts and then re-assembled these into a (doubtless unseaworthy) ship. Does this have a better claim to be the original ship of Theseus? There is

The ship is made of the wood.

vagueness of some kind here. The question is: is the ship *itself* vague, or does the vagueness end with the word "ship", leaving the ship itself uncontaminated?

It seems to me that the second answer is the right one. In such a case, we can give an agreed and relatively precise account of the "facts of the matter". We know just what happened. It is a verbal question to which object, if any, we ought to apply the phrase "the ship of Theseus". So the vagueness comes from words.

This view could be supported by a two-stage argument. First, show that *identity* is not a vague relation; that is, show that questions of the form "Is this thing (perhaps, Theseus's original ship) the same as that thing (perhaps, the ship later reassembled from the parts of Theseus's original)?" have definite answers. The suggestion is that, quite generally:

If β is α, then β is definitely α; and if β is not α, then β is definitely not α.

Suppose β is α. It seems indisputable that, for any object x,

x is definitely x.

So "is definitely α" is true of α. If β is α, anything true of α is true of β. So "is definitely α" is true of β. Hence:

β is definitely α.[22]

The second stage of the argument involves showing that if identity is not a vague relation, then objects are not vague. The idea is that if an object were vague, it would be a vague matter what object it is identical with. Since the first part of the argument has supposedly shown that identity is not vague, the conclusion is drawn that objects are not vague.

I close with four qualms.

First, the second step of the argument is not cogent as stated. It is not unreasonable to suppose that, if there are any vague objects, collections with vague membership conditions are included. So if there are uniformly coloured blocks of various colours and weights on my table, including various red ones and orange ones, the collection of red blocks on my table has a vague membership condition, and for some block, it may be a vague matter whether it belongs to the collection or not. The collection seems as good a can-

---

22 Can you establish the rest of what is needed for the non-vagueness of the identity relation, viz.:

if β is not α, then β is definitely not α?

Cf. Evans (1978), Wiggins (1986).

didate as any for being a vague object. Yet we might insist that the identity conditions for such collections are completely precise. If we ask whether the collection of red blocks is the same collection as the collection of heavy blocks, we might insist that an affirmative answer requires that the collections coincide in every respect: all the definite members of the red collection must be definite members of the heavy collection and vice versa, all the definite non-members of the red collection must be definite non-members of the heavy collection and vice versa; and so on through any further distinctions. There would then never be any vagueness about whether this collection is the same as or different from that collection. We thus have not excluded the possibility of vague objects without vague identity.

Secondly, denying that there are vague objects seems to presuppose that the "facts themselves" are precise. I said that, in the case of Theseus's ship, the facts of the matter are "relatively precise". They are precise relative to the vagueness of "ship", since they can be stated without using that word. However, other words, like "plank", have to be used. This is just as vague as "ship". Can we be sure that there is a range of ultimate facts that can be described without using any vague expressions at all? Such a belief would surely need very careful justification.

The third qualm is this: identity over time, as discussed in the case of the ship, must surely be governed by principles like: replacing some, but not too many, parts of an artefact does not destroy it, but leaves you with the very same artefact. Such principles are vague. How could the identity relation, which they determine, be precise?[23]

The final qualm is more technical: the best implementation I know of the semantic approach mentioned at the end of the previous section, in which a vague language is used to describe vagueness, posits the existence of vague objects, namely, vague sets. This might give one a starting point from which to extend belief in vague objects more widely.

---

[23] How would you evaluate the following argument?
If you exist at all, you are a vague object, for we believe that a molecule more or less cannot make the difference between whether you exist or do not. On this basis, we can construct a paradoxical argument: taking away one molecule will not make you cease to exist, taking away one more will not make you cease to exist, and so on; thus you can exist even if no molecules of you do. This shows that you are as vague as a heap. However, there are no vague objects, therefore you do not exist.
See Unger (1979b).

Bibliographical notes

Section 2.1
An introductory article is Black (1937); see also Dummett (1975). For an interesting attempt to identify a common cognitive source of paradoxes see Sorensen (1988). The best comprehensive study of vagueness is Williamson (1994). For a survey of treatments of sorites paradoxes, see Sainsbury and Williamson (1995).

For an argument for the utility of vagueness, see Wright (1975). For his more recent views see Wright (1987).

Section 2.3
For the view that there are no tables, see Unger (1979a).

Section 2.4
For the epistemic theory, see Cargile (1965), Sorensen (1988), Sainsbury and Williamson (1995), Williamson (1992b, 1994). I say that this view has "*re*surfaced", because it can be traced back to Chrysippus (c. 280 – c. 207 B.C.).

Section 2.5
A classic text for the supervaluation theory is Fine (1975); see also van Fraassen (1966); Kamp (1975). These papers involve some technicalities. For a less formal account of the underlying idea, see Dummett (1975, esp. pp. 256–7). For a brief history, a critical discussion, and a development of the theory to accommodate higher order vagueness, see Williamson (1994). For the relation between supervaluation theory and higher order vagueness, see also Fine (1975, esp. §5).

The criticism of supervaluation theory given in the text, that it verifies the intuitively unacceptable "For some number n, an n-grained collection is a heap but an $(n-1)$-grained collection is not", has been attacked. Various writers have suggested that the quoted sentence is acceptable, as long as we realize that its truth does not require that there be a number n such that the following is true:

> an n-grained collection is a heap but an $(n-1)$-grained collection is not.

See, e.g., Dummett (1975, pp. 257–8); and, for opposition, Kamp (1981, pp. 237ff.). The claim depends upon two features: (1) a view of "there is" according to which it is like "or" (so that to say that there is a student who smokes is to say that either Sally smokes, or Michael smokes, or …, and so on through all the students); and (2) a view of "or" according to which a statement "p or q" can be (definitely) true even though neither "p" nor "q" is. A standard alleged example of the latter is "This is orange or red", said of a borderline case. See again Dummett (1975, p. 255). It is not at all clear whether the combination of (1) and (2) is less paradoxical than the paradox of the heap. It involves claiming that "there is a such-and-such" can be true, even if "that is a such-and-such" is false of each thing in the universe.

For higher order vagueness, see Wright (1992) and the symposium between Hyde (1994) and Tye (1994b).

Section 2.6
A classic source for degree theory is Zadeh (1965). I had mostly in mind the kind of theory advanced in Goguen (1969). For a version which does not treat the connectives as degree functional see Sanford (1975). For a more philosophical and less technical account of degree theory, see Peacocke (1981). For criticisms see Edgington (1992), Sanford (1976), and, on the resulting logic, Fine (1975), and Williamson (1994). For an account of validity and degrees according to which modus ponens remains valid, see Edgington (1992).

For the notion of partial belief, see Ramsey (1926) and Jeffrey (1965, chapters 3 and 4). A substantive question is whether a similar argument could be used to underwrite objective probabilities. If the answer is affirmative, as Mellor (1971) argues, then a question of crucial importance would be whether one can give a satisfactory account of why the arguments reach different destinations: degrees of truth in one case, objective probabilities in the other. Edgington (1992) suggests that less than full confidence induced by vagueness behaves differently from less than full confidence induced by lack of information.

For a semantics with a vague metalanguage, see Tye (1994a).

Section 2.7
On vague objects, see Evans (1978), Lewis (1988), Nathan Salmon (1982, pp. 243ff.), Tye (1990) and Wiggins (1986).

3. Acting rationally

3.1 Newcomb's paradox

You are confronted with a choice. There are two boxes before you,
A and B. You may either open both boxes, or else just open B.
You may keep what is inside any box you open, but you may not
keep what is inside any box you do not open. The background is
this.

A very powerful being, who has been invariably accurate in his
predictions about your behaviour in the past, has already acted in
the following way:

> He has put $1,000 in box A.
> If he has predicted that you will open just box B, he has in
> addition put $1,000,000 in box B.
> If he has predicted that you will open both boxes, he has put
> nothing in box B.

The paradox consists in the fact that there appears to be a decisive
argument for the view that the most rational thing to do is to open
both boxes; and also a decisive argument for the view that the most
rational thing to do is to open just box B. The arguments commend
incompatible courses of action: if you take both boxes, you cannot
also take just box B. Putting the arguments together entails the
overall conclusion that taking both boxes is the most rational thing
and also not the most rational thing. This is unacceptable, yet the
arguments from which it derives are apparently acceptable.

The argument for opening both boxes goes like this. The powerful being – let us call him the Predictor – has already acted. Either
he has put money in both boxes or he has put money in just box A.
In the first case, by opening both boxes you will win $1,001,000.
In the second case, by opening both boxes you will at least win
$1,000, which is better than nothing. By contrast, if you were to
open just box B, you would win just $1,000,000 on the first

assumption (i.e., that the Predictor has put money in both boxes) and nothing on the second assumption (i.e., that the Predictor has put money just in box *A*). In either case, you would be $1,000 worse off than had you opened both boxes. So opening both boxes is the best thing to do.

The argument for opening just box *B* goes as follows. Since the Predictor has always been right in his previous predictions, you have every reason for thinking that he will be right in this one. So you have every reason to think that if you were to open both boxes, the Predictor would have predicted this and so would have left box *B* empty. So you have every reason to think that it would not be best to open both boxes. Likewise, you have every reason to think that if you choose to open just box *B,* the Predictor will have predicted this, and so will have put $1,000,000 inside. Imagine a third party, who knows all the facts. He will bet heavily that if you open just box *B* you will win $1,000,000. He will bet heavily that if you open both boxes you will get only $1,000. You have to agree that his bets are rational. So it must be rational for you to open just box *B*.

This paradox has been used to compare two different principles for determining how it is rational to act. One principle is this: act so as to maximize the benefit you can expect from your action. In stating this principle, "benefit" is usually replaced by the technical term "utility". Part of the point of the technical term is to break any supposed connection between rationality and selfishness or lack of moral fibre. A benefit or "utility" consists in any situation that you want to obtain. If you are altruistic, you may desire someone else's welfare, and then an improvement in his welfare will count as a utility to you. If you want to do what is morally right, an action will attract utility simply by being in conformity with what, in your eyes, morality requires, even if from other points of view, say the purely material one, the consequences of the action are not beneficial to you.

There is obviously something appealing in the principle that it is rational to act so as to *maximize expected utility* – MEU for short. Consider gambling: the bigger the prize in the lottery, the more money it is rational to pay for a ticket, everything else being equal; the larger the number of tickets, the less money it is rational to pay. The MEU principle tells you to weigh both these factors. If there are 100 tickets and there is just one prize of $1,000, then you will think that you are doing well if you can buy a ticket for less than $10. (If you could buy them *all* for less than $10 each, then you could be certain of gaining $1,000 for an expenditure of less than $1,000.) If the tickets cost more than $10, you may have to think of the lottery as a way of raising money for a charity that you wish to support, if you are to buy a ticket.

Such an example contains a number of quite unrealistic assumptions. Some of these are inessential, but at least one is essential if the MEU principle is to compare any possible pair of actions for their degree of rationality. This is the supposition that utilities and probabilities can be measured.[1,2,3] If they can, then we can simply compute which of the actions open to us have greatest expected utility: we multiply the measure of utility by the measure of the probability of that utility accruing.

Lotteries are useful examples of how probability can be measured. If a lottery is fair, each ticket has an equal chance of winning: the chance for any ticket in an n-ticket lottery winning is simply $1/n$. Probability theorists generalize this notion in the following way. Suppose that there are just x relevant and exclusive possibilities (e.g. that ticket number 1 is the unique winner, that ticket number 2 is the unique winner, and so on), and that of these y have the property P (e.g. that the winning ticket is mine). Then the probability that what actually happens has property P (e.g. that my ticket wins) is given as y/x. This means that the highest measure of probability is 1 (when $x=y$, e.g., if I buy all the tickets) and the lowest 0 (if $y=0$, e.g. if I buy no tickets), with the intermediate measures lying in between.

Lotteries are also useful examples of how utilities can be measured, if we allow ourselves the simplifying assumption that the cash value of the win represents its utility. So we can readily use

---

1   Suppose that on Monday you are penniless and starving, but that on Tuesday you win $1,000,000 in a betting pool. Do you think that the number 5 can be used to measure the utility of $5 to you on each of these days?

2   Suppose you have four courses of action open to you, (a)–(d), associated with rewards as follows: (a) $1, (b) $6, (c) $10,000, (d) $10,005. Do you think that the number 5 can be used to measure both the difference between the utilities of (a) and (b) and the difference between the utilities of (c) and (d)?

3* Discuss the following view:
    Although people want things other than money, we can nevertheless use numbers to measure how much they want things, by finding out how much they would be willing to pay, supposing, perhaps *per impossibile*, that what they want could be bought. If a man says he wants a happy love affair, we can measure the utility of this upshot to him by finding out how much money he would be willing to give up to get what he wants. Would he give up his car? His house? His job? All that is needed is the ability to imagine things being other than they are: to imagine that things that in fact cannot be bought can be bought.

lotteries to exemplify expected utility. Suppose that there are two lotteries, one with 1,000 tickets and a single $1,100 prize, and one with 900 tickets and a single $1,000 prize. Expected utility is the chance you think you have of winning times the utility of the win. For the first lottery this can be represented as $1/1,000 \times 1,100 = 1.10$. For the second, it can be represented as $1/900 \times 1,000 = 1.11$ (approx.). The expected utility of the second lottery is a shade higher than that of the first. So if the tickets for both lotteries cost the same, and you are going to buy a ticket for one, the MEU principle recommends that you choose the second.

The MEU principle does not recommend that you buy a ticket in either lottery. There may well be many alternative ways of spending your money with expected utilities higher than those associated with either lottery. The principle only tells you that *if* you are going to buy a ticket for either, it should be for the second.[4]

The notion of utility was introduced in terms of what upshot an agent wants. What someone wants sometimes means what he or she wants all things considered. If I decide to go to the dentist, then typically I want to go – that is, want to go all things considered. However, what a person wants can also mean anything to which he attaches some positive value. In this sense, it is true of me, when I freely and willingly go to the dentist, that I want not to go: not going has the positive value of sparing time and present discomfort. If I go, it is because this want is trumped by another: I want to avoid decay, and for the sake of that benefit I am prepared to put up with the loss of time and the discomfort. The appropriate connection between utility and wanting should exploit not what an agent wants overall, but rather that to which he attaches any positive value.

The situation that gives rise to Newcomb's paradox can be represented as shown in Figure 3.1. The expected utility of opening both boxes is calculated as follows. By the background of the problem, you regard it as very likely that the Predictor will have correctly predicted your choice. Hence if you open both boxes you must think that it is very likely that the Predictor will have predicted this and so will have put no money in box *B*. So the expected utility is some high ratio close to 1, call it *h*, measuring the likelihood of this outcome, multiplied by 1,000, measuring the utility. Analogously, the expected utility for you of opening just box *B* is the same high ratio, measuring the likelihood of the Predictor having correctly predicted that this is what you would do, and so hav-

---

[4]* Could the MEU principle register a general dislike of gambling, as opposed to other ways of spending money? If so, how?

ing put $1,000,000 in box *B*, multiplied by 1,000,000, measuring the utility of that outcome. Since, whatever exactly *h* may be, $1,000 \times h$ is much less than $1,000,000 \times h$, MEU recommends opening just box *B*.

	The Predictor has *not* put money in *B*	The Predictor *has* put money in *B*
you open *A* and *B*	$1,000	$1,001,000
you open just *B*	$0	$1,000,000

Figure 3.1: Newcomb's paradox.

I will set out the calculations in more detail. (Readers who feel they have a good enough hang of them should skip to the next paragraph.) The expected utility of an action is calculated as follows. First, you determine the possible outcomes O_i. Each is associated with a probability, conditional upon doing *A*, and a utility. The expected utility of an *outcome*, relative to an action *A*, is the product of its utility and its probability given *A*. The expected utility of an action *A* is the sum of the expected utilities of its outcomes relative to *A*:

$$EU(A)=[\text{prob}(O_1/A).U(O_1)] + [\text{prob}(O_2/A)\ U(O_2)] + \ldots$$

Here "$EU(A)$" stands for the expected utility of *A*, "$\text{prob}(O_i/A)$" for the probability of outcome O_i given *A*, and "$U(O_i)$" for the utility of that outcome. Applied to Newcomb's paradox, using *B* for the action of opening only box *B*, and *A&B* for the action of opening both boxes, we have:

$EU(B) = [\text{prob}(B \text{ is empty}/B).U(B \text{ is empty})] + [\text{prob}(B \text{ is full}/B).U(B \text{ is full})] = (1-h).0 + h.1,000,000.$

$EU(A\&B) = [\text{prob}(B \text{ is empty}/A\&B).U(B \text{ is empty and } A \text{ is full})] + [\text{prob}(B \text{ is full}/A\&B).U(B \text{ is full and } A \text{ is full})] = h.1,000 + [(1-h).1,001,000].$

Setting $h = 0.9$ makes $EU(B) = 900,000$ and $EU(A\&B) = 101,100$, giving a nearly ninefold advantage to taking just box *B*.

The MEU principle underwrites the argument for opening just box *B*. To resolve the paradox, however, one would need to show what was wrong with the other argument, the argument for opening both boxes. Those who are persuaded that it is rational to open both boxes will regard the fact that the MEU principle delivers the contrary recommendation as a refutation of the principle.

One attractive feature of MEU is that it is a quite general, and independently attractive, principle. Are there any other principles of rational action that are also attractive, yet that deliver a different recommendation? There are. One example is the so-called *dominance principle* – DP for short.

According to DP, it is rational to perform an action α if it satisfies the following two conditions:

(a)   Whatever else may happen, doing α will result in your being no worse off than doing any of the other things open to you.

(b)   There is at least one possible outcome in which your having done α makes you better off than you would have been had you done any of the other things open to you.

DP has commonsensical appeal. If you follow it you will act in such a way that nothing else you could do would have resulted in your faring better, except by running the risk of your faring worse.

Figure 3.1 may be taken to show that opening both boxes satisfies DP, and that opening only box *B* does not.[5] Whatever the Predictor has done, you are better off opening both boxes than opening just one. In either case, you stand to gain an extra $1,000 as compared with the other course of action open to you. Hence DP and MEU conflict: they commend opposite courses of action.

One way to diagnose Newcomb's paradox is precisely as the manifestation of this conflict of principle. The constructive task is then to explain how the principles are to be restricted in such a way that they cease to conflict, while retaining whatever element of truth they contain.

How is the Predictor so good at predicting? Suppose it worked like this. Your choice would cause the Predictor to have made the correct prediction of it. To take this alleged possibility seriously, we have to take seriously the possibility of "backward causation": that is, a later event (here your choice) causing an earlier one (here the Predictor's prediction). Let us for the moment take this in our

---

[5]*   Suppose that we think of the outcomes in a different way, as shown in the following table:

	The Predictor has predicted correctly	The Predictor has predicted incorrectly
you open *A* and *B*	$1,000	$1,001,000
you open just *B*	$1,000,000	$0

Opening both boxes appears no longer to dominate opening just one box. How should one respond?

stride. If one knew that this was how things worked, surely there could not be two views about what it would be rational to do. One should open just box *B,* for this would cause the Predictor to predict that this is what one would do, which would lead to his having put $1,000,000 in box *B.* Not making this choice, by contrast, would lead to his not having put the $1,000,000 in box *B.* Clearly it would be crazy not to choose to open just box *B.*

The original case was, perhaps, underdescribed. Perhaps it did allow for the possibility (if there is such a possibility) of backward causation. To prevent confusion, let us stipulate that the *original case* is one that excludes backward causation. It is instructive, however, to consider this *other* case, where there is supposed to be backward causation. Perhaps the attraction of opening just box *B* in the original case sprang from thinking of it as the backward causation case. More generally, perhaps the paradox strikes us as paradoxical only to the extent that we confuse the original case with the backward causation case. To the extent that we think of the case as involving backward causation, we are tempted by MEU. To the extent that we think of it as excluding backward causation we are tempted by DP. What strikes us as conflicting views of the same case are really views of different cases.

In the original case, one might suppose that the Predictor bases his decision on general laws, together with particular past facts. These might all be physical, or they might be psychological. For example, the laws might be laws of psychology, and the particular facts might concern your personality. There is no question of backward causation. Then the basis for the prediction consists in facts that lie in the past. Rejecting backward causation, this means that nothing you can now do can affect the basis for the prediction. Hence nothing you now do can make any difference to whether there is or is not money in box *B.* So you should open both boxes.

There is a complicating factor. Suppose that determinism is true. Suppose, in particular, that the psychological laws, together with data about your character up to the time at which the Predictor made his prediction, determine how you will now act, in the sense of making it impossible for you to do anything other than what, in fact, you will do. This may totally undermine the idea of rational decision, and so make the whole question of what is best to do one that cannot arise. In short, there is a case for saying that if there were such a Predictor, then there could be no question about which choice is rational. I shall ignore this case, and argue that it is rational to open both boxes. Those who are moved by it could read my conclusion as hypothetical: if we can make sense of rationality at all in the deterministic Newcomb situation, then the rational thing is to open both boxes.

In defending this conclusion, I need to consider whether, as claimed earlier, it is rational for the onlookers to bet heavily on the following two conditionals:

(a)   if you select both boxes, box *B* will be empty;

(b)   if you select just box *B,* it will contain $1,000,000.

If they are rational, the onlookers will bet in accordance with their expectations. Their expectations are the same as yours. They have very strong reason to believe the two conditionals, given the Predictor's past successes. How can this be reconciled with my claim that if the Predictor bases his prediction on past evidence, then it is rational to open both boxes? If it is rational for the onlookers to expect the conditionals to be true, it must be rational for you to expect the same. However, you have a *choice* about which conditional will count. It is rational, surely, to make the second conditional count, and you can do this by opening just box *B*. How can one reconcile the rationality of belief in the conditionals with the rationality of opening both boxes?

Let us look more closely at the basis of the rationality of belief in the conditionals. We can do this by looking at it from the point of view of the onlookers. They reason as follows. The Predictor has always been right in the past. Since he has already filled the boxes, his prediction is based on knowing some past facts about you and your circumstances, and applying some generalizations. Our best evidence for what he has predicted is what you choose to do. This is why we believe the conditionals. Your opening just box *B* is evidence that the Predictor has predicted this and, hence, by the way the problem is set up, is evidence that he has filled box *B* with $1,000,000. Likewise for the other possibility.

The rationality of these beliefs does not entail the rationality of opening just box *B*. This is most easily seen if we switch to the subject's point of view: to *your* point of view, as we are pretending. The Predictor makes his choice on the basis of past facts about you, together with some generalizations. To simplify, let us say that there are two relevant possible facts about what sort of person you were at the time the Predictor made his prediction: either you were a one-boxer – that is, a person disposed to open just box *B* – or you were a two-boxer – that is, a person disposed to open both boxes. If you find yourself tempted to open both boxes, that is bad news.[6] It is evidence that you are now a two-boxer and, all other

6   How would you respond to the following argument?

things being equal, is thereby evidence that you were a two-boxer at the time when the Predictor made his decision. Hence it is evidence that he will have predicted that you will open both boxes, and so it is evidence that there will be no money in box *B*. However, there is no point in trying to extirpate this disposition, and it would be a confusion to think that you could make any difference to the situation by resisting it. There is no point trying to extirpate it *now,* since the Predictor has made his prediction and either he noticed your two-boxing disposition or he didn't. If he did notice it, getting rid of it now is closing the stable door after the horse has bolted. Nothing you can now do can make any difference as to whether or not you were a two-boxer at the time the Predictor made his prediction. Thus it can be rational to open both boxes even if it is also rational to believe that if you open both boxes, box *B* will probably be empty. It is rational to believe this conditional because it is rational to believe that if you open both boxes you are a two-boxer, and if you are now a two-boxer you probably were one when the Predictor scanned you, in which case he has probably predicted that you will open both boxes, in which case he has probably not put anything in box *B*.

If you found in yourself an inclination to open just box *B,* that would be good news, for analogous reasons; but it is an inclination that it would be more prudent to resist. By resisting it and opening both boxes, you cannot make the money that you can reasonably presume is already in box *B* go away, and you will gain the extra $1,000 in box *A*.

Here is an objection. If this is where the reasoning were to end, would not a really good Predictor have predicted this, and therefore have ensured that there is nothing in box *B*? Furthermore, had you taken the reasoning through a further twist, using the fact just mentioned as a reason for in the end taking just box *B,* the Predictor would have predicted this too, and so would have filled box *B*. So is not this what you should do?

However, the original difficulty remains and cannot be overcome. No matter what twists and turns of reasoning you go in for now, you cannot affect what the Predictor has already done. Even if you could make yourself now into a one-boxer, it would not help. What mattered was whether you were a one-boxer, or a per-

---

It would come as wonderful news to learn that I am a one-boxer, for then I will be able to infer that I will soon be rich. However, I can give myself that news simply by deciding to be a one-boxer. So this is what I should decide to do.

son likely to become a one-boxer, at the time when the Predictor made his prediction. You cannot change the past.[7,8]

We have said that the Predictor has *always* been right in the past.[9] Let us imagine, in particular, that he has always been right about Newcomb problems. We shall suppose that each person is confronted with the problem only once in his life (there is no second chance), and that the Predictor has never been wrong: never has a two-boxer found anything in box *B,* and never has a one-boxer found box *B* empty. Most of your friends have already had the chance. The one-boxers among them are now millionaires. You wish above all things that you were a millionaire like them, and now your chance has come: you are faced with the Newcomb problem. Is it not true that all you have to do is choose just box *B*? Is that not a sure-fire way to riches? So how could it be rational to refuse it?

So far, this raises no new considerations: the two-boxer's reply still stands. However, I have put the matter this way in order to add the following twist. Being of good two-box views, you think that the Predictor is, for some crazy reason, simply rewarding irrationality: he makes one-boxers rich, and one-boxers are irrational. Still, if you want to be rich above all things, then is not the *rational* thing to do to join the irrational people in opening just box *B*? Sir John Harington (1561–1612) wrote that

> Treason doth never prosper; what's the reason?
> For if it prosper, none dare call it treason.

Likewise, if "irrationality" pays, then it is not irrationality at all! You want to be rich like your millionaire friends, and if you think as they do you will be. It is rational to adapt means to ends, so it is rational to think the way they think.

---

[7] We have envisaged the choice before you being a once-in-a-lifetime chance. However, suppose you knew that you were going to be allowed to make this choice once a week for the rest of your life, and suppose the facts about the Predictor remain the same. What is the most rational policy to pursue?

[8] Consider a variant of the problem – let us call it the "sequential Newcomb". The difference is that you are allowed to make your choice in two stages: you can elect to open box *B*, reserving your choice about box *A* until you find out what is in box *B*. Suppose you open *B* and there is nothing inside. Should you elect also to open *A*? Suppose you open *B* and there is $1,000,000 inside. Should you elect also to open *A*? Do your answers have any implications for the original Newcomb?

[9] Consider a variant in which he has *mostly* been right in the past. Would this make any difference to the argument? Try working out what the MEU recommends if we set the probability of the Predictor being right at 0.6.

This suggestion can be represented as involving two main points. The first is that one might reasonably want to be a different sort of person from the sort one is: here, a less rational sort. Some people committed to lucidity and truth as values find this suggestion unpalatable.[10] However, a second point is needed: that if it is reasonable to want to be a different sort of person, then it is reasonable, even as things are, to act as that other sort of person would have acted. The second point is what secures the passage from envying the one-boxers to the claim that it would be rational to follow their lead. Once clearly stated, this second point can be seen to be incorrect: given that you are not a "natural" one-boxer, given that you are persuaded by the argument for two-boxing, nothing can as things stand make it *rational* for you to one-box. (Quite likely, most of us would succumb to irrational forces and one-box, but that does not show we would be rational to do so.)

A clear perception of the advantages of being a one-boxer cannot give you a *reason* for becoming one – even if that were in your power. Atheists might clearly perceive the comfort to be derived from theism, but this does not give them a *reason* for believing that God exists. The light of reason cannot direct one toward what one perceives as irrational. To adopt a position one regards as irrational one needs to rely on something other than reason: drugs, fasting, chanting, dancing, or whatever.[11]

This way of dealing with the paradox takes no account of the two principles, MEU and DP. Is either to be accepted? MEU cannot be correct, since it commends taking just box *B*. DP cannot be correct since, in the other version of the paradox, in which backward causation was admitted, DP wrongly recommended taking both boxes.[12,13] However, we may be able to see why the

10 What are your own views on this point? Some people say that they wish they could believe in life after death. If this wish involves wishing that they could cease to be moved by the evidence *against* life after death, it is an example of the sort of desire whose reasonableness or rationality is in question.

11 Would you feel differently if there was just $1 in box A (with the same arrangements for box B)? Would you feel differently if there was $900,000 in box A (with the same arrangements for box B)? Cf. Nozick (1993, p. 44–5).

12 Consider some familiar gambling game (e.g., roulette or poker). Can DP be used to say which bets in your selected game are rational? Assume that the only aim is to win as much money as possible.

13 Israel is wondering whether to withdraw from territories it occupies. Egypt is wondering whether or not to go to war with Israel. From Israel's point of view, the utilities are as follows:

principles let us down when they did, and this may lead to ways of suitably restricting them.

In the backward causation case, it is no accident that DP gives the wrong result. It has no means of taking into account the fact that your choice will affect what is in the boxes, by affecting the Predictor. More generally, it gives the wrong result because it makes no provision for the ways in which one's acting can affect the probabilities of outcomes. The backward causation case alone shows that DP cannot serve as it stands as a universally correct principle of rational action: it cannot be rational to act in such a way as to cause a diminution in the likelihood of someone else doing something that would increase one's benefits.

Equally, it is no accident that MEU gives the right result for the backward causation case. The rationale of MEU is given by the thought that it is rational to act in ways one takes to be likely to *promote* one's benefits. In the backward causation case, one has reason to believe that how one acts will affect one's benefits by affecting the Predictor's decision. In this case, the conditional probabilities reflect the probability of one's action genuinely promoting one rather than another outcome.

By contrast, this does not hold in the original case. The conditional probabilities obtain, but in a way that fails to reflect the underlying rationale of the MEU. The probability that if you open both boxes, box *B* will be empty is indeed high; but it is not high because your opening both boxes will have any causal role in bringing it about that box *B* is empty. The right restriction on MEU, so far as Newcomb's paradox goes, is that one should act on the principle only when the conditional probabilities reflect what one believes one's actions will *produce*.

We have seen that DP is not an acceptable principle of rational action, since it takes no account of conditional probabilities. This fact explains why it happens to give the right result in the original case. Here, because the probabilities are irrelevant, in that they do not reflect the likely effects of the possible actions, it is right to ignore them. So far as this case goes, one appropriate restriction on DP is that it can be used only when there is no relevant difference in the probability of the various possible outcomes.

	Egypt declares war	Egypt does *not* declare war
Israel withdraws	0	2
Israel remains	1	3

Show how this example can be used to demonstrate that DP does not always give correct results. (See Bar-Hillel and Margalit 1972.)

Though these considerations explain away Newcomb's paradox, they leave a great deal of work to be done within the wider task of understanding the nature of rational action. A first point to consider would be whether the modified versions of MEU and DP are *consistent*: whether, that is, they would deliver the same account for all cases of how it is rational to act.[14] One would have to go on to ask whether they are *correct*: whether either delivers for all cases a correct account of how it is rational to act. It is unlikely that any such simple principles would be adequate to this task. Indeed, many philosophers are sceptical concerning many of the notions upon which this discussion has been based. It is not at all plausible to think that the values that are at issue in deciding what to do are measurable in the way that has been presupposed. It would be important to consider whether any substantive principles of rationality can be formulated that do not rest on this supposition. A wider issue is whether we have any right to a supposedly objective, culture-independent notion of rationality as a scale against which any action at all can be measured. Perhaps there are species of rationality, or perhaps rationality is simply one value among others. In the next section, I consider one alleged threat to the coherence of the notion of rationality.

[14] How would you respond to the following argument?

The dominance principle DP cannot conflict with the MEU principle, if by this is meant that there is a situation in which an action with maximum expected utility would fail to be preferred by the dominance principle. For any upshot, the probability of its occurring is the same regardless of the action, so the only relevant fact, for each upshot, is the utility. So MEU and DP cannot diverge. The table makes this plain:

	P_1	P_2
A_1	5	2
A_2	4	2

A_1 and A_2 are actions open to you. The possible outcomes are P_1 and P_2. If you do A_1 and P_1 is the outcome, your utility is measured by the number 5. Likewise for the other cells in the table. The dominance principle commends A_1 in preference to A_2. The MEU either does likewise or else is indifferent between A_1 and A_2, and in either case the principles do not conflict. To show this, let us call the agent's probabilities of P_1 and P_2 respectively π_1 and π_2 . We do not know what these values are, but we can be sure that $5 \times \pi_1$ is greater than $4 \times \pi_1$, and that $2 \times \pi_2$ is not greater than $2 \times \pi_2$. So MEU must either recommend A_1 or else be neutral.

3.2   The Prisoner's Dilemma

You and I have been arrested for drug running and placed in separate cells. Each of us learns, through his own attorney, that the district attorney has resolved as follows (and we have every reason to trust this information):

(1)   If we both remain silent, the district attorney will have to drop the drug-running charge for lack of evidence, and will instead charge us with the much more minor offence of possessing dangerous weapons. We would then each get a year in jail.

(2)   If we both confess, we shall both get five years in jail.

(3)   If one remains silent and the other confesses, the one who confesses will get off scot-free (for turning State's evidence), and the other will go to jail for ten years.

(4)   The other prisoner is also being told all of (1)–(4).

How is it rational to act? We build into the story the following further features:

(5)   Each is concerned only with getting the smallest sentence for himself.

(6)   Neither has any information about the likely behaviour of the other, except that (5) holds of him and that he is a rational agent.

There is an obvious line of reasoning in favour of confessing. It is simply that whatever you do, I shall do better to confess. For if you remain silent and I confess, I shall get what I most want, no sentence at all; whereas if you confess, then I shall do much better by confessing too (five years) than by remaining silent (ten years). We can represent the situation by Figure 3.2, and the reasoning in favour of confessing is the familiar dominance principle (DP).

	you confess	you don't confess
I confess	<5,5>	<0,10>
I don't confess	<10,0>	<1,1>

Figure 3.2: The Prisoner's Dilemma.

In the figure <0,10> represents the fact that on this option I go to prison for zero years, and you go for ten years; and so on. The smaller the number on my (left) side of the pair, the better I am pleased. It is easy to see that confessing dominates silence: confessing, as compared to silence, saves me five needless years if you confess, and one if you do not.

Since you and I are in relevantly similar positions, and, by (6), we are both rational, presumably we shall reason in the same way, and thus perform the same action. So if it is rational for me to confess, it is rational for you to do likewise; but then we shall each go to prison for five years. If we both remain silent, we would go to prison for only one year each. By acting supposedly rationally, we shall, it seems, secure for ourselves an outcome that is worse for both of us than what we could achieve.

On this view, rational action in some circumstances leads to worse outcomes than other courses of action. Even if this is depressing, it is not as it stands paradoxical: we all know that irrational gambles can succeed. What is arguably paradoxical is that the case is one in which the failure of rationality to produce the best results is not a matter of some chance intervention, but is a predictable and inevitable consequence of so-called rational reasoning. How, in that case, can it be rational to be "rational"? (Compare: how could it be rational to be a two-boxer, if being a one-boxer would ensure that one would be a millionaire?) The allegedly unacceptable consequence of the apparently acceptable reasoning is that rational action can be seen in advance to make a worse outcome highly likely.

If this is a paradox, then the correct response, I believe, is to deny that the consequence is really unacceptable. The unacceptability is supposed to consist in the fact that if we were both to act in a certain way, we would be better off than if each were to follow the supposed dictates of rationality. Hence rationality is not the *best* guide to how to act, in that acting in the other way would lead to a better outcome for both. The trouble with this suggestion is that any guide to action has to be available to the agent's decision-making processes. To be guided by the thought that we would both be better off if both remained silent than if both confessed, I would need to know that you would remain silent. What it is rational to do must be relative to what we know. If we are ignorant, then of course acting rationally may not lead us to the best upshot. Here, the ignorance of each concerns what the other will do; and this, rather than some defect in rationality, is what yields the less than optimal upshot.

However, we are now close to a paradox of a different sort. I have said that there is a compelling argument for the rationality of confessing. Yet it appears that there is also a strong case for the rationality of remaining silent. If this case is good, then two apparently acceptable arguments lead to conclusions that, taken together, are unacceptable.

The argument for silence goes like this. We both know we are rational agents, because that is built into the story. We therefore know that any reason one of us has for acting will apply to the other. Hence we know that we shall do the same thing. There are two courses of action that count as doing the same thing: both confessing or both remaining silent. Of these, the latter is preferable for both of us. So of the available courses of action, it is obvious which each of us must rationally prefer: remaining silent.

This argument invites a revenge. Suppose silence is the rational choice, and that I know it is. Then, in knowing that you are rational, I know that it is the choice you will make. So I know that you will remain silent. However, in that case it must be rational for me to confess, thus securing my preferred outcome: getting off scot-free. On the other hand, I know that you can reason like this too; therefore, if you are rational, you will not keep silent. In that case it is again – but more urgently – rational for me to confess. The way of silence is unstable. Thus the hypothesis that keeping silent is the rational choice is refuted.

The previous paragraph undermines the argument for the claim that silence is the rational policy, and thus removes the threatened paradox that both silence and confession are the rational policy. We should not, however, be content with simply showing this: we should ask how the case connects with the principles of rational action already discussed.

The MEU principle, as stated in section 3.1, claimed that the rational act was whatever maximized expected utility, where this was to be understood in terms of two factors: the desirability of a certain outcome and its probability, conditional upon the performance of a given act. In connection with Newcomb's paradox, I originally said that the relevant probabilities were

(a)   the probability of there being $1,000,000 in box *B*, *given that* I choose to open both boxes, and

(b)   the probability of there being $1,000,000 in box *B*, *given that* I choose to open just box *B*.

In the discussion, I claimed that these are not the right probabilities to consider if they do not reflect the tendency of my action to *produce* the outcome in question. So what are the right probabilities to consider? One suggestion is that they are (a′)   the probability of my bringing it about that there will be $1,000,000 in box *B* by choosing both boxes, and

(b′)   the probability of my bringing it about that there will be $1,000,000 in box *B* by choosing one box.

Assuming that there is no backward causation, both of these probabilities are 0. If we stipulate that anything known to be true anyway (having a probability of 1, regardless of my action) is something that *anything* I do counts as bringing about, then opening box *A* has an expected utility equal to the utility of $1,000, and opening only box *B* has an expected utility of 0. The version of MEU that considers the probabilities (a′) and (b′), rather than (a) and (b), supports two-boxing.

Let us apply the contrast between these two versions of MEU to the Prisoner's Dilemma. The probability of you confessing, given that I confess, is high and equal to the probability of you remaining silent, given that I remain silent. Moreover, the probability of you confessing, given that I remain silent, is low, and so is the probability of the converse. These conditional probabilities follow from my knowledge, built in to the example, that you and I will reason in similar ways, since we are both rational.[15] With suitable utilities, there will be versions of the dilemma in which MEU, in its original form, designates silence as the rational course of action.[16]

In its modified form, MEU was to take into account the probability of an action *producing* the relevant outcome. Since that probability is by stipulation 0 in the present case, because each of us makes his decision before knowing what the other has decided, the modified MEU does not give us any guidance: all the expected utilities, understood in this way, are the same. However, this fact would be a telling reason for applying DP: if you have no idea what outcomes your actions will bring about, choose that action that will make things better for you whatever the other person does.

---

[15] Clarify the assumption behind the remark that if two people are rational, then for any problem both will reason about it in similar ways. Is the assumption justifiable?

[16] Using the numbers in Figure 3.2 as the utilities of the various outcomes (prefix each with a minus sign to show that the outcomes are mostly undesirable), how could you assign conditional probabilities (using numbers between 0 and 1) in such a way as to make the expected utility of silence higher than that of confession? Your assignment will justify the sentence in the text.

It has been suggested that Newcomb's paradox is simply a version of the Prisoner's Dilemma. In Newcomb's paradox, the crucial matter – whether or not there is anything in box *B* – is one of match: the money is in the box if and only if my action matches the prediction. It does not matter whether the prediction occurs before or after the act of choice; what matters is that the act of choice should have no effect on the content of the prediction. Likewise, match is of the essence in the Prisoner's Dilemma: knowing that we are both rational, I expect my action to match yours, just as I expect the prediction to match my choice. Moreover, just as I cannot affect the prediction, so I cannot affect your choice. Figure 3.3 sets out the similarities.

		silent one box	confess two box
X	confess two box	1	3
Y	silent one box	2	4

Figure 3.3: Similarities between Newcomb's paradox and the
Prisoner's Dilemma.

I have to choose whether to do *X* (confess, take both boxes) or *Y* (remain silent, take just one box). The column indicates what the other character in the story may do: the other prisoner remains silent or confesses; the Predictor predicts that I shall one-box or else that I shall two-box. My preferences among the outcomes, from best to worst, are in this order: 1, 2, 3, 4. The "matching possibilities" are shaded: the other prisoner does what I do, the Predictor predicts correctly. I know that my choice cannot affect whether or not a match will occur. I know that a match is much more likely than a mismatch.

In a nutshell, the two arguments we have considered are these:

(A)   Do *X,* since you are better off, whatever the other does, than you would be if you were to do *Y:* 1 is better than 2, and 3 is better than 4.

(B)   Do *Y,* since match is the most likely kind of outcome, and of these 2 is better than 3.

If this analogy is correct, then one has *consistent* views on the problems only if one is either a two-boxer and a believer in confessing, or else a one-boxer and a believer in silence. My view is the first.

The Prisoner's Dilemma is a simplified version of a well-known conflict: if co-operating means forgoing something that one would otherwise have preferred, then co-operation appears not to be in one's best interests. What serves my purposes best is to secure co-operation from you, while not being co-operative in return. In the Prisoner's Dilemma, what would be best for me is that you remain silent, perhaps under the influence of persuasion, threats, or promises from me, while I, perhaps reneging on undertakings to you, confess. If the first view is correct, and X-ing is the rational thing to do, then if we both pursue our interests rationally, we shall end up serving these interests less well than we might. This is not really unacceptable, for it is true; but it may seem depressing.

In the case we have considered, there is just a single situation requiring a decision. Suppose instead that we are confronted with a "multiple Prisoner's Dilemma": suppose that there are a series of choices, and that we each know this – in particular, we each know that this is not the last time we shall be playing the game with each other – and that we also know that the other will remember, and no doubt be guided by, what has happened on previous occasions. There is an argument to the effect that this new situation would push me in the direction of silence. Suppose you get the idea that I am the sort of person who generally confesses. Then I know that this will make you confess too, to protect yourself from the disastrous consequences of silence, and the overall result will be less than the best for me, time after time. So I have an interest in getting you to believe that I am the sort of person who generally remains silent. One way I can propagate this view is by in fact remaining silent. (We all know, from our knowledge of used car salesmen and politicians, that this is not the only way to try to achieve this kind of effect.) I also know that you will follow the same policy. So in this situation the co-operative policy of silence would appear to be the rational one.[17]

There is fascinating evidence that this is not far from the truth. In some computer simulations of Prisoner's Dilemma situations, the following strategy did better than any other: start by remaining silent; thereafter do what the other player did on the previous round. In suitable circumstances, this will lead to a situation of stable co-operation. Since the multiple Prisoner's Dilemma corresponds more closely to more of real life than the single case, it may be that the upshot of the discussion ought not to be so depressing:

[17*] Suppose that all parties know in advance how many times they will be in this situation – fifty times, say. How would you state the case for the view that the most rational policy is always to confess?

perhaps rational self-interest is not doomed to lead to a non-optimal outcome.

Bibliographical notes

Newcomb's paradox (also known as Newcomb's problem) first appeared in print in Nozick (1969). Nozick says that the paradox was invented by Dr William Newcomb of the Livermore Radiation Laboratories in California. As far as I know, Newcomb himself has not written about his paradox. Nozick (1993) makes new contributions to the discussion of this paradox and the general issues which it raises.

The discussions to which I am most indebted are Mackie (1977) and Gibbard and Harper (1978). For a defence of one-boxing see Bar-Hillel and Margalit (1972).

On probability see Ramsey (1926), Jeffrey (1965); and, for wider applications, Kyburg (1961) and Levi (1967).

Hollis and Sugden (1993) provide a good recent overview of many of these issues. See also Campbell (1985) for a useful collection of essays and a good editor's introduction.

Systematic studies of rational decision include Jeffrey (1965) and Anand (1993).

A response to Newcomb's paradox not explored in the text is this: the arguments for one-boxing and for two-boxing are equally compelling, but inconsistent, so there can be no such Predictor (compare, there can be no such Barber). See Schlesinger (1974b) and a critical discussion by Benditt and Ross (1976).

For a discussion of what probabilities should properly be considered in rational action, taking causation into account, see Gibbard and Harper (1978).

The issues raised by the Prisoner's Dilemma connect closely with practical problems: see e.g. Parfit (1984, chapters 2–4).

For the similarity between Newcomb's paradox and the Prisoner's Dilemma see Lewis (1979). For a similar problem, see Selton (1978).

For an account of the results of computer simulation of various strategies for playing multiple Prisoner's Dilemma games, see Axelrod (1984).

4.   Believing rationally

This chapter concerns problems about knowledge or rational belief.
The first main section, called "Paradoxes of confirmation", is about
two paradoxes that might be called "philosophers' paradoxes". Let
me explain.

Most of the paradoxes in this book are quite straightforward to
state. Seeing what is paradoxical about them does not require any
special knowledge – you do not have to be a games theorist or a
statistician to see what is paradoxical about Newcomb's paradox or
the Prisoner's Dilemma, nor do you have to be a physicist or
sportsman to see what is paradoxical about Zeno's paradoxes. By
contrast, the paradoxes of confirmation arise, and can only be understood, in the context of a specifically philosophical project.
Therefore these paradoxes need some background (section 4.1.1)
before being introduced (in sections 4.1.2 and 4.1.3). The background section sets out the nature of the project within which the
paradoxes arise.

The last three main sections of the chapter (4.2–4.4) concern the
paradox of the Unexpected Examination. Although it is hard to resolve, one form of it is easy enough to state. (More complex
forms, discussed in sections 4.3–4.4, involve technicalities: these
sections can be omitted without loss of continuity.) This paradox
has been used to cast doubt on intuitively natural principles about
rational belief and knowledge.

4.1   Paradoxes of confirmation

4.1.1   Background

We all believe that there is a firm distinction between strong, good,
or reliable evidence on the one hand, and weak, bad, or unreliable
evidence on the other. If a stranger at the racetrack tells you that
Wolf-face will win the next race, and you have no other relevant

information, you would be a fool to bet heavily on Wolf-face. The evidence that he will win is extremely thin. However, had the trainer given you the same tip, that would have provided you with much stronger evidence. It would be stronger still if you knew that the trainer was a crook who believed that you were on to him, and if you also knew that he thought a good tip would buy you off.

Most of our actions are guided by scarcely conscious assessments of how good our evidence is for certain of our beliefs. When we choose what film to see or what restaurant to patronize we are often guided by past experience: by whether the director or actors have good track records, or whether the restaurant has produced good food in the past. We are also guided by what other people say: we weigh their testimony, trusting some – good reviewers, or people we know to be good judges of food – more than others. In such everyday cases, our assessment of the quality of the evidence is unreflective: we recognize good judges and bad judges, good signs and bad signs; but we never normally ask ourselves what *constitutes* a good judge or a good sign.

The philosophical project within which the paradoxes of section 4.1 arise is to state general principles determining what counts as good evidence. Such principles sometimes surface outside philosophy departments. In law courts, for example, explicit categorizations of the evidence ("circumstantial", "inadmissible") are used to grade it; and in scientific investigations, in particular those involving certain kinds of numerically structured data, there are elaborate and sophisticated statistical theories bearing on the question of the extent to which data support a hypothesis.

The branch of philosophy in which philosophers have tried to articulate general principles determining the quality of evidence is called "confirmation theory". These attempts have given rise to surprising paradoxes. Understanding them will lead to a better idea of the nature of evidence.

If a body of propositions constitutes *some* evidence (however slight) for a hypothesis, let us say that these propositions *confirm* the hypothesis. From this starting point one might hope to develop an account of what one should believe. For example, one might think that one ought to believe, of all the relevant hypotheses that one can conceive, those best confirmed by all of one's data. Be that as it may, there are problems enough even with the starting point, let alone what one might develop from it.

A very natural thought is that the following principle will play some fundamental role in an account of confirmation:

G1   A generalization is confirmed by any of its instances.

Here are some examples of generalizations:

(1)   All emeralds are green.

(2)   Whenever the price of cocaine falls, its consumption rises.

(3)   Everyone I have spoken to this morning thinks that the Democrats will win the next election.

(4)   All AIDS victims have such-and-such a chromosome.

G1 asserts that these propositions are confirmed by their instances – that is, respectively, by this, that, or the other emerald being green; by cases in which the price of cocaine falls and its consumption increases; by the fact that I spoke to Mary this morning, and she thinks that the Democrats will win; and by the fact that Frank, who has AIDS, also has this chromosome. G1 does not assert, crazily, that an instance can *establish* a generalization. A single instance can *confirm,* according to G1, but obviously that does not settle the matter. A single instance does not even show that it is rational to believe the hypothesis, let alone that it is true.

I have spoken both of objects (like emeralds) and of facts (like the fact that Frank has AIDS and also this chromosome) as instances of generalizations, and I shall continue to do so. However, on state occasions I shall say that an instance of a generalization is itself a proposition. When the generalization has the form

All *A*s are *B*s,

an *instance* of it is any proposition of the form

This *A* is a *B*.

Thus

This emerald is green

is an instance of

All emeralds are green.

A *counterinstance* of a generalization "All *A*s are *B*s" is a proposition of the form

This *A* is not a *B*.

So

This emerald is not green

is a counterinstance of "All emeralds are green". Just as we may, on non-state occasions, speak of green emeralds as instances of this latter proposition, so we can speak of non-green emeralds as counterinstances of it.

The opposite of confirmation is *disconfirmation*. A hypothesis is disconfirmed by propositions that tend to show it to be false. An extreme case is *falsification*: a generalization is falsified by any counterinstance of it.

The principle G1 is to be understood to mean that any proposition that is an instance of a generalization confirms that generalization. It is not always clear how this is meant to link up with the notion of good evidence. Obviously, one AIDS victim with a certain chromosome does not alone constitute good evidence for the hypothesis that all AIDS victims have it; but perhaps a large number of instances, and no counterinstances, do add up to good evidence. If so, we shall think of each instance as making a positive contribution to this good evidence, and this is what people have in mind by the notion of confirmation. G1 does not say, absurdly, that an instance of a generalization would, in and of itself, give us good reason to believe that generalization. Rather, it says that an instance makes a positive contribution, however slight, and however liable to be outweighed by other factors, toward constituting good evidence. The idea is that if we know of an instance of a generalization, we have taken one small step toward having good evidence for that generalization, even though other things we know may undermine this evidence. Indeed, our other knowledge might include a counterinstance of that same generalization.

The quality of evidence is a matter of degree. Some evidence is stronger, other evidence weaker. One way we might try to build toward this from the idea of confirmation, together with G1, is by saying that your evidence for a generalization is stronger the more instances of it your total body of knowledge contains – provided that it contains no counterinstances. However, one must beware of supposing that it is at all easy to arrive at a correct account. The following shows that what has just been suggested is indeed wrong. One could well have come across many instances, and no counterinstances, of the generalization

All places fail to contain my spectacles

(one has searched high and low without success); yet one would be quite right to be certain that this generalization is false.

The appeal of G1 comes in part from the thought that *extrapolation* is reasonable. If all the things of kind *A* that you have examined have also been of kind *B,* then you have some reason to extrapolate to the hypothesis that all things of kind *A* are of kind *B*. Of course, the evidence may be slight, and it may be outweighed by other evidence.

We are not usually interested in confirmation (in the technical sense used here) in cases of generalizations such as "Everyone I met this morning said that the Democrats would win". If I had met a reasonably small number of people, I might say in the afternoon: "I don't need evidence – I already *know* that it's true". The idea is that my own experience already determines the truth of the generalization. The contrast is with generalizations such as "Whenever the price of cocaine falls, its consumption increases". You may know that this has held so far, but this does not settle that the proposition is true, for it speaks to future cases as well as past ones. This is the sort of generalization for which we feel we need evidence: a generalization not all of whose instances one has encountered.[1]

Inductive reasoning, as philosophers call it, consists in arguing from evidence or data to hypotheses not entailed by these data. One traditional philosophical problem has been to justify this process: to show that it is at least sometimes legitimate to "go beyond the data". Let us call this the problem of *justification.* Another philosophical problem is to give a general account of the kinds of inductive reasoning we *take* to be legitimate (without necessarily pronouncing on whether or not they are really legitimate). Let us call this the problem of *characterization.* We take it that it is legitimate to argue from the fact that the sun has risen every day so far to the conclusion that it will, probably, rise every day in the future; or, at least, to the conclusion that it will, probably, rise tomorrow. By contrast, we do not think that it is legitimate to argue from these same data to the conclusion that the sun will sometime cease to rise, or to the conclusion that it will not rise tomorrow.[2] The problem of characterization is to give an illuminating general account of the features of evidence that make us count it as *good* evidence, as a legitimate basis for the hypothesis in question.

An initial answer to the problem of characterization is that inductive reasoning is generally taken to be legitimate when it is a case of extrapolation: when one reasons on the assumption that what one has not experienced will resemble what one has. G1 is

[1] There are generalizations of which one could not be sure that one had encountered all the instances. What are some examples?

[2] Victims of the so-called Monte Carlo fallacy dispute this. They hold that the longer the run of successive reds on a fair roulette wheel the *less* likely it is that red will come up on the next spin. What, if anything, is wrong with this view? Is there anything right about it?

connected with this initial suggestion, for it specifies a way of extrapolating.

These problems of induction are akin to problems already encountered. Earlier, we asked "Under what conditions are data good evidence for a hypothesis?" If we can answer this question in some illuminating way (and not merely by saying, for example, "When they are"), we shall thereby be close to having solved the problem of justification – for we shall then be close to showing that it *is* sometimes legitimate to go beyond the data.[3] Moreover, if we could answer the question "Under what conditions are data *taken to be* good evidence for a hypothesis?", we would have answered the problem of characterization.

We shall be concerned only with the characterization problem: not the question of whether there is any genuinely legitimate inductive reasoning, but rather the question of what sort of inductive reasoning we (rightly or wrongly) take to be legitimate. Though this seems the easier problem, attempts to answer it lead quickly to contradictions.

4.1.2   The paradox of the Ravens

Despite the initial appeal of G1, it leads, in conjunction with other apparently innocuous principles, to a paradox discovered by Carl Hempel (1945), and now generally known as the paradox of the Ravens.

In order to derive the paradoxical consequence, we need just one other principle:

> **E1**   If two hypotheses can be known *a priori* to be equivalent, then any data that confirm one confirm the other.

This needs some explanation. Something can be known *a priori* if it can be known without any appeal to experience. For example, one does not have to conduct any kind of social survey to discover that all women are women: indeed, one could not discover this by a survey. What can be known *a priori* can be known simply on the basis of reflection and reasoning.

Two hypotheses are equivalent just on condition that if either one is true, so is the other, and if either one is false, so is the other. E1 asks us to consider cases in which two hypotheses can be

---

[3]* How might answering this question fail to show that inductive reasoning is sometimes legitimate, and thus fail to be a complete answer to the problem of justification?

known *a priori* to be equivalent. An example would be the hypotheses

R1   All ravens are black

and

There are no ravens that are not black

and also

R2   Everything non-black is a non-raven.

Any two of these three hypotheses are equivalent, and this can be shown simply by reflection, without appeal to experience; so the equivalence can be known *a priori*. For example, suppose R1 is true: all ravens are black. Then, clearly, any non-black thing is not a raven, or, as R2 puts it, is a non-raven. So if R1 is true, so is R2. Now suppose that R1 is false; then some ravens are not black. However, this means that some things that are not black are not ravens, so R2 is false, too. Thus R1 and R2 are equivalent, and this can be known *a priori*.

We can now show how the paradox of the Ravens is derived from G1 and E1. By G1, R2 is confirmed by its instances – for example, by a white shoe, or (using the state-occasion notion of an instance) by, for example:

P1   This non-black (in fact, white) thing is a non-raven (in fact, a shoe).

Instance P1 confirms R2, but R2 can be known *a priori* to be equivalent to R1. So, by E1, P1 confirms R1, "All ravens are black". This, on the face of it, is absurd. Data relevant to whether or not all ravens are black must be data about ravens. The colour of shoes can have no bearing whatsoever on the matter. Thus G1 and E1 – apparently acceptable principles – lead to the apparently unacceptable conclusion that a white shoe confirms the hypothesis that all ravens are black. This, finally, is our paradox.

The principles of reasoning involved do not appear to be open to challenge, so there are three possible responses:

(a)   to say that the apparently paradoxical conclusion is, after all, acceptable;

(b)   to deny E1; or

(c)   to deny G1.

Hempel himself makes the first of these responses. One could argue for it as follows. First, we must bear in mind that "confirm" is being used in a technical way. It does not follow from the supposition that a white shoe *confirms* that all ravens are black that observing a white shoe puts you in a position reasonably to believe that all ravens are black. Second, there are cases in which it seems quite natural, or at least much less absurd, to allow that P1 confirms that all ravens are black – that is, that P1 could make a positive contribution to some good evidence for the hypothesis. Suppose that we are on an ornithological field trip. We have seen several black ravens in the trees and formulate the hypothesis that all ravens are black. We then catch sight of something white in a topmost branch. For a moment we tremble for the hypothesis, fearing a counterinstance – fearing, that is, that we have found a white raven. A closer look reveals that it is a shoe. In this situation, we are more likely to agree that a white shoe confirms the hypothesis. Hempel tells a similar story for a more realistic case. Investigating the hypothesis that all sodium salts burn yellow, we come across something that does not burn yellow. When we discover that the object is a lump of ice, we regard the experiment as having confirmed the hypothesis.

The first point appeals to the idea that some complicated story must be told in order to link confirmation to having good reason to believe. Furthermore, in the telling, it will be apparent why observing white shoes, despite their confirmatory character with respect to the hypothesis that all ravens are black, does not normally contribute to giving one good reason to believe the hypothesis. We cannot assess the suggestion until we know the details of this story.

The second of these points emphasizes that confirmation, as we normally think of it, is not an absolute notion but is relative to what background information we possess. Making this point leaves unstarted the task of specifying how the technical notion of confirmation – which, so far, has been taken as absolute – should be modified so as to take account of this relativity.

Perhaps these points can be developed so as to justify the first response, (a); but I shall now turn to the other possible responses.

Response (b) is to deny E1. For example, one might simply insist that anything that confirms a generalization must be an instance of it. This avoids the paradox, but it is very hard to justify. For example, suppose that we are investigating an outbreak of Legionnaires' disease. Our hypothesis is that the source of the infection was the water at St George's school, consumed by all the children who attended last week. Will only an instance of the generalization "All pupils attending St George's last week contracted Legionnaires' disease" confirm it? Imagine that we find some St George's children who are free from the disease, but that it then turns out that they missed school last week. We would normally count this as evidence in favour of our hypothesis – some potential and highly relevant counterinstances have been eliminated – and yet these children are not instances of the hypothesis.

There is a more general argument against the rejection of E1. Suppose we find some data that confirm two hypotheses, H1 and H2. It is standard practice to reason as follows: H3 is a consequence of H1 and H2, so to the extent that H1 and H2 are confirmed, so is H3. For example, if we had data that confirmed both the hypothesis that all anorexics are zinc-deficient and the hypothesis that everyone who is zinc-deficient is zinc-intolerant, the data would surely confirm the hypothesis that all anorexics are zinc-intolerant. However, if we allow that data confirm the *a priori* knowable consequences of hypotheses they confirm, we have in effect allowed E1.[4]

The third possible response to the paradox is to reject G1. This is both the most popular response, and also, I believe, the correct one. The paradox of the Ravens already gives us some reason to reject it, if the other responses are unsatisfactory. The paradox of "grue", to be considered in the next section, gives a decisive reason for rejecting it. Moreover, there are quite straightforward counterexamples to it. Consider, for example, the hypothesis that all snakes inhabit regions other than Ireland. According to G1, a snake found outside Ireland confirms the hypothesis; but however we pile up the instances, we get no evidence for the hypothesis. Quite the contrary: the more widespread we find the distribution of snakes to be, the more unlikely it becomes that Ireland is snake-free. A non-Irish snake does not confirm the hypothesis, since it makes no positive contribution to the evidence in favour of the hypothesis, and may even count against it.

Rejecting G1 resolves the paradox, but it leaves us in a rather unsatisfactory position regarding confirmation. We have made very little progress toward uncovering the principles that underlie our discrimination between good and bad evidence. The next paradox brings to light more difficulties in the path of this project.

4.1.3 *"Grue"*

According to G1, green emeralds confirm the hypothesis that all emeralds are green. Now consider the predicate "grue", invented by Nelson Goodman (1955) with an eye to showing the inadequacy of G1. The meaning of "grue" is stipulated so as to ensure

---

4 How does this follow?

that a thing x counts as *grue* if and only if it meets either of the following conditions:

Gr1 x is green and has been examined, or
Gr2 x is blue and has not been examined.

The class of grue things is thus, by definition, made up of just the examined green things together with the unexamined blue things. All examined emeralds, being all of them green, count as grue, by Gr1. It follows from G1 that the hypothesis that all emeralds are grue is confirmed by our data: every emerald we have examined is a confirming instance because it was green. This is absurd. If the hypothesis that all emeralds are grue is true, then unexamined emeralds (supposing that there are any) are blue. This we all believe is false, and certainly not confirmed by our data. G1 must be rejected.

What is paradoxical is that a seeming truth, G1, leads, by apparently correct reasoning, to a seeming falsehood: that our data concerning emeralds confirm the hypothesis that they are all grue.[5] The paradox relates to the problem of *characterization* – of saying what kinds of evidence we take to be good, or what sorts of inductive argument we take to be legitimate – because we need to say what makes us treat green and grue differently. G1 does not discriminate between the cases.

The conclusion is unacceptable even if we recall that "confirms" is being used in a technical sense: it is not equivalent to "gives us good reason to believe", but means only something like "would make a positive contribution to a good reason for believing". It strikes us as unacceptable to suppose that an examined green emerald makes any contribution at all to giving a good reason for supposing that all emeralds are grue.

We have already seen in connection with the Ravens (section 4.1.2) that there is a case for rejecting G1; that case is, of course, strengthened by the present Grue paradox. If we reject G1, then both paradoxes are, for the moment, resolved, for we shall have said that an apparently acceptable premise is not really acceptable. However, what can we put in its place? It would seem that something like G1 must be true. Is there an appropriate modification? If not, then the Grue paradox remains not fully resolved; for to say

[5]*   An alternative presentation of the paradox identifies the apparently unacceptable conclusion as being that the same body of data can confirm the *inconsistent* hypotheses that all emeralds are green and that all emeralds are grue. Is it unthinkable that a body of data should confirm inconsistent hypotheses?

that there is no appropriate modification of G1 is to say that there are no principles governing what makes a body of data confirm a hypothesis. This seems as unacceptable as the view that green emeralds confirm the hypothesis that all emeralds are grue.

Several suggestions have been made. Most of them can be seen as falling into one of two patterns:

(1)   The blame is placed on the word "grue", which is said to be of a particularly nasty or "pathological" kind, rather than on the structure of G1. All we need is a general principle for excluding the *grue*-some words, and G1 will be acceptable for the remainder.

(2)   The blame is placed not so much on "grue" as on the attempt to formulate a principle, like G1, that takes no account at all of *background information* – information that is always in play in any real-life case of evidence or confirmation.

If we try the first response, the difficulty is to say exactly what is nasty about "grue". It is not enough to say that "grue" is an invented word, rather than one that occurs naturally in our language. Scientists often have to invent words (like "electron") or use old words in new ways (like "mass"), but it would be extravagant to infer that these new or newly used words cannot figure in confirmable generalizations.

It is more appealing to say that what is wrong with "grue" is that it implicitly mentions a specific time in its definition. Its definition appeals to what has *already* been examined, and this refers to the time at which the definition is made. In this respect, "grue" and "green" differ sharply, for there is no *verbal* definition of "green" at all, and even if there were it would certainly not involve reference to a particular time.

If we were to restrict G1 to generalizations in which there is no reference to a time, it would be too restrictive. For example, the generalization "In Tudor times, most agricultural innovations were made in the north of the country" is one that could be confirmed or disconfirmed on the pattern of G1. In addition, G1 would not be restrictive enough. The structure of the Grue paradox is preserved if we can find a way of picking out just the emeralds we have already examined. We might do this by giving each one a name, e_1, e_2, ...; or it might be that all and only the emeralds so far examined have come from a certain emerald mine (now exhausted); or something of the kind. Then we could define a predicate equivalent to "grue" without mentioning a time. We could say that it is to apply to any of e_1, e_2, ...just on condition that that thing is green, and to anything else just in case it is blue; or we could say that it is to apply to everything taken from a certain mine just on condition that it is green, and to anything else just on condition that it is blue. Therefore it is not of the essence of the paradox that the definition of "grue" mentions a time.

There are other ways of trying to say what is nasty about "grue". Goodman's own attempt has at least superficial similarities with one I rejected earlier. He says that what is wrong with "grue" is that it is not "well-entrenched"; that is, the class of entities to which it applies is a class that has not been alluded to much – indeed, at all – in the making of predictions (see Goodman 1955, esp. pp. 97ff). To treat being poorly entrenched as sufficient for being incapable of figuring in confirmable generalizations seems to put an intolerable block on scientific innovativeness. Though Goodman is well aware of this problem, and provides a more sophisticated response than my brief description would suggest, there is room for doubt about whether he deals with it successfully.

I now want to consider a response of the other kind I mentioned: not restricting G1 by limiting it to generalizations that do not contain words sharing the supposed nasty features of "grue", whatever these features may be; but rather restricting G1 by appeal to background information. Intuitively, what is wrong with supposing that our information about examined emeralds gives us any reason for thinking that all emeralds are grue is that we know that the examined ones are grue only in virtue of having been examined. We do not believe that our examining the emeralds had any "real" effect on them. We believe that if they had not been examined they would not have been grue. What makes it so absurd to suppose, on the basis of our data, that all emeralds are grue is that we know that the unexamined ones lack the property in virtue of which the examined ones *are* grue: namely, having been examined. An initial attempt to formulate this thought might look like this:

> G2   A hypothesis "All *F*s are *G*s" is confirmed by its instances if and only if there is no property *H* such that the *F*s in the data are *H,* and if they had not been *H,* they would not have been *G.*

We might try to support G2 by the following case, which in some respects looks similar to the grue emeralds. Suppose that we are gathering evidence about the colour of lobsters, but unfortunately we have access only to boiled ones. All the lobsters in our sample are pink. Moreover, we know that the lobsters in the sample are pink only in virtue of having been boiled. Then it would be absurd for us to think that our sample confirms the hypothesis that all lobsters are pink. Here the hypothesis is "All lobsters (F) are pink (G)", and H is the property of having been boiled. Because the lobsters in the sample are boiled, and had they not been boiled would not have been pink, the data do not meet the condition imposed by G2 for confirming the hypothesis (Jackson 1975).

The lobster case brings to light a difficulty, or series of difficulties, connected with G2. We start to uncover them if we ask: how do we know that the lobsters in the sample would not have been pink had they not been boiled? It would seem that if we know this, then we know that some lobsters are not pink at all times, and thus we are in a position to know that the hypothesis is false.

This shows that we can explain, without appealing to G2, why the evidence for the hypothesis that all lobsters are pink was deficient. A body of evidence fails to confirm any hypothesis to which it contains a counterinstance. However, the case in addition brings to light something more fundamental: that G2, as it stands, does not require our *body of data* to contain the proposition that there is no H such that the examined Fs would not have been G had they not been H. It requires only that this proposition be true. What would be relevant to G2 would thus be a variant of the lobster case in which all observed lobsters are pink, but we, the observers, do not realize that they are pink only because they have been boiled. G2 rules that, in this state of ignorance, our data do not confirm the generalization that all lobsters are pink. Is this acceptable?

This raises an important issue. If it sounds wrong to say that the person who has observed only pink lobsters, and who knows nothing of the connection between boiling and colour (and perhaps does not even know that the sample lobsters have been boiled), lacks data that would confirm the hypothesis that all lobsters are pink, this is because we intuitively feel that evidence should be *transparent*. By this I mean that we intuitively feel that if a body of data is evidence for a hypothesis, then we ought to be able to tell that this is so merely by examining the data and the hypothesis: one ought, in other words, to be able to tell that this is so *a priori*. This intuitive feeling might be supported by the following argument. Suppose that no evidence is, in this sense, transparent. Then, a claim to the effect that a body of data D confirms a hypothesis H will itself be a hypothesis needing confirmation. We shall need to cast around for data to confirm, or disconfirm, the hypothesis that D confirms H. It looks as if we are set on an infinite regress, and that we could never have any reason to suppose that anything confirms anything unless evidence is transparent.

Not all evidence is transparent. Spots can confirm the hypothesis that the patient has measles, but one needs medical knowledge to recognize that the data, the spots, are thus related to the hypothesis: one needs to know that only people, or most people, with spots of this kind have measles. In other words, it is clear that in many cases the evidence is not transparent. In any case, the most the argument of the preceding paragraph could show is that *some* evidence needs to be transparent, since this is all that is needed to block the alleged regress.

If we feel that some evidence should be transparent, we shall surely feel that an example is the limiting case in which everything that *can* be included among the data *has* been included. In this case, we shall feel that one ought to be able to tell *a priori*, without further investigation, which hypotheses these data confirm. However, this is not guaranteed by G2, for two reasons.

First, for some hypotheses of the form "All Fs are Gs", our data may include plenty of instances and no counterinstances but fail to contain either the proposition "There is no H such that all examined Fs are H and would not have been G had they not been H" or its negation. In this case, if G2 is true, we could not tell *a priori* whether our data confirm the hypothesis, since we could not tell whether the condition it places on the instances of the hypothesis obtains or not.

Second, it is a debatable question whether this condition *could* properly be included among our data. One might hold that all data must, in the end, be observations, and that a condition such as "There is no H such that all examined Fs are H and would not have been G had they not been H" is not immediately available to observation, and so cannot be a datum.

These objections point in controversial directions. The second objection presupposes a form of *foundationalism,* which is highly controversial. Perhaps, contrary to the presupposition, there is nothing in the intrinsic nature of a proposition that qualifies it as a datum or as a non-datum; thus, on occasion, the counterfactual condition could count as a datum. If this is allowed, then we could envisage a variant of G2 that meets the first of the two objections.

G3   A hypothesis "All Fs are Gs" is confirmed by a body of data containing its instances, and containing no counterinstances, if and only if the data do not say, of some property H, that the Fs in the data are H, and if they had not been H they would not have been G.

This rules that "All emeralds are grue" is not confirmed by its instances, for our data do say, concerning the property *being examined,* that the emeralds in the data have been examined, and had they not been examined they would not have been grue. It has the further merit of being consistent with transparency: whether or not a body of data confirms a hypothesis depends only on the data and the hypothesis themselves, and not on other, perhaps inaccessible, facts. However, it has the apparently dubious feature that smaller bodies of data can confirm more than can larger bodies.

To see how this works, imagine two people, both confronted with pink boiled lobsters, and both concerned to consider the question of whether their data confirm "All lobsters are pink". One person does not realize that all the lobsters he has seen have been boiled, or else does not realize that boiling them affects their colour. If G3 is correct, that person's data do confirm the hypothesis "All lobsters are pink". The other person, by contrast, knows that the lobsters would not have been pink had they not been boiled. G3 entails that that person's data do not confirm the hypothesis that all lobsters are pink. If you know more, your data may confirm less.

This feature is one that should come as no surprise. A body of data full of instances of a generalization, and containing no counterinstances, may confirm the generalization, though the same body enriched by a counterinstance would not. Still, G3 needs refinement. For one thing, it still leads, in conjunction with E1, to the Ravens paradox.[6] For another thing, we need to modify it somewhat in the light of examples like the following.

Suppose you find, year after year, that although all the other vegetables in your garden are attacked by pests, your leeks are always pest-free. Would it be reasonable to conclude that leeks are immune to pests? Let us suppose that you know no proposition to the effect that your leeks would not have been pest-free had they not possessed some property *P*. According to G3, the hypothesis that all leeks are immune to pests is confirmed by your data; but I think that we should not, in fact, put much confidence in the hypothesis, given the data. Even if one knows no proposition of the relevant kind, one may strongly suspect that *there is* one, even though one does not know it. One knows in a general way that susceptibility to pests is likely to be affected by such factors as the nature of the soil, how strongly the plant grows, and what other vegetation is around. Even though your data do not include a proposition that selects a factor that explains the pest-free quality of

[6] Sketch a proof of the Ravens paradox, using G3 rather than G1.

your leeks, you might well believe that *there is* a proposition of this kind. If so, you should not put much faith in the hypothesis that all leeks, including those grown in very different conditions, are immune to pests.

If it is to deliver the results we want in such cases, G3 would need to be revised, so that:

> **G 4**   A hypothesis "All *F*s are *G*s" is confirmed by a body of data containing its instances, and containing no counterinstances, if and only if the data do not say that *there is*, or even that *there is quite likely to be*, a property, *H*, such that the examined *F*s are *G* only in virtue of being *H*.

All other things being equal, the fact that we think it quite likely that there are conditions under which leeks suffer from pests is enough to diminish, or even perhaps cancel, the confirmatory impact of our pest-free leeks; G4 is intended to do justice to this fact.

G4 entails that the hypothesis that all emeralds are grue *is* confirmed by the data consisting just of propositions of the form "This is a green emerald", "This has been examined", and so on; but it does not entail that this hypothesis is confirmed by the body of data, including background information, that we in fact possess. That body of data includes the proposition that the examined emeralds would not have been grue had they not been examined; so it entails that there is a property (*having been examined*) such that the emeralds in the data are grue only in virtue of possessing that property.

Does G4 rule out enough?[7] One might in particular have doubts about whether it should allow that the grue hypothesis is confirmed by the narrower body of data. These doubts might be to some extent assuaged by reflecting that a body of data can confirm a hypothesis that they do not make it rational to believe. We could insist that sometimes instances confirm, in the sense of making a positive contribution to good grounds for belief, while not on their own constituting such grounds.

The following example is designed to put this view to the test. We have to try to imagine a case in which we have just the

---

[7]   What are the advantages (if any) and disadvantages (if any) of the following variant (call it G5)?

A hypothesis "All *F*s are *G*s" is confirmed by a body of data containing its instances, and containing no counterinstances, if and only if the data say that no property, *H*, is such that the *F*s in the data are *H*, and if they had not been *H* they would not have been *G*.

instances of a generalization, and absolutely no relevant background information at all. Suppose you come across a very large sack of marbles. You cannot see into the sack, but you manage to take out one marble at a time. You do this for a while, and all those you take out are green. By G4, the hypothesis that all the marbles are green, including the unseen ones still in the sack, is confirmed. However, I claim that you still do not have good reason to believe that all the marbles in the sack are green. The case is, by stipulation, one in which you are not allowed to bring to bear any background information in the form of suppositions about how the marbles came to be in the sack. The hypothesis that they were put there by a collector of marbles must be, for you, no more likely than that they were put there by a philosopher wanting to make a point about confirmation theory. Moreover, you can form no reasonable belief about whether you are, or are not, selecting the marbles "at random". Perhaps the only way to extract a marble is to press a lever at the side of the sack. You have no idea whether they are being dealt from the top or in some other order, or whether the mechanism selects them in some genuinely indeterministic fashion. Under these circumstances, it seems to me quite doubtful whether the run of green marbles gives us good grounds for believing that all the marbles in the sack are green. In particular, there does not seem to be much difference in the justification of the view that they are all green and the view that they are all grue. It must be stressed that such situations are bound to be rare. Perhaps we have to imagine ourselves on an alien planet, governed by unknown physical laws, to ensure that we are really not bringing background information to bear, as we normally would.

We perhaps incline to think that if *all* we knew about emeralds consisted in a large number of green samples, it is not merely that the hypothesis that all emeralds are green would be confirmed by our data: in addition, we would be justified in believing it. This, I think, is an illusion. In forming this view, I think we unconsciously bring to bear background information concerning the colour constancy of most gemstones, together with the supposition that emeralds are gemstones. Take this supposition away, and there can be no move from confirmation to justified belief. One can see this by comparing the case in which all the tomatoes I have ever come across are green. This would give me good reason to believe that all tomatoes are green only if I had good reason to think that the sample tomatoes were somehow typical; but of course I can have no such reason.

I claim that G4 will remove anything puzzling about the Grue paradox. It explains how, as things are, our data do not confirm that all emeralds are grue; and although it concedes that other, narrower bodies of data might confirm this generalization, it would be reasonable to make the further claim that, in this case, confirmation falls short of good grounds for belief. However, as should be obvious from the rest of the discussion, this leaves a great deal to be said about the nature of confirmation and its ultimate connection with the notion of rational belief.

The Grue paradox has been held to have more distant ramifications. To gesture toward these, let us consider a corollary that Goodman stresses:

> Regularities are where you find them, and you can find them anywhere.

The old idea – found, for example, in Hume – was that to reason from experience in a way we take to be legitimate is to extrapolate regularities obtaining within our experience. One thing that Goodman's "grue" shows is that this is, at best, a highly incomplete account, for it does not answer the question: what is a regularity? The regular connection between being an emerald and being green? *And* the regular connection between being an emerald and being grue? Our original problem re-emerges in this form: either we can give no account of what a regularity is, in which case it is useless to describe our inductive practice as extrapolating experienced regularities; or else we give an account of regularity that includes the undesirable emerald–grue regularity as well as the desirable emerald–green one.

This relatively narrow point about confirmation suggests a deeper metaphysical one: that whether a series of events counts as a regularity depends upon how we choose to describe it. This has suggested to some a quite thoroughgoing conventionalism, according to which there is no separating how the world is in itself from the conventions we bring to bear in describing and classifying it. To others, it has had the effect of deepening their scepticism about the legitimacy of inductive reasoning. If there are endless regularities that we could have extrapolated, what makes it rational to pick on the ones we in fact do? It is bad enough having to justify extrapolating a regularity, but it is worse when one must, in addition, justify selecting one rather than any of the countless other regularities in the data to extrapolate. To yet others, the Grue paradox has suggested that there is something quite undetermined, at least at the individual level, about our concepts. Wittgenstein asked us to consider someone who, having added 2 to numbers all the way up to 1,000, continues this way – 1,004, 1,008, ... – and yet protests that he is "going on in the same way". We could define a gruelike operator "+*" as follows: $x +^* 2 = x + 2$, if $x < 1,000$; otherwise $x +^* 2 = x + 4$. It has been suggested that there are no facts, or at least no individual facts, that make it true of us that we use concepts like *green* and $+$ rather than concepts like *grue* and $+^*$.

The impact of grue goes well beyond the problems of finding a non-paradoxical account of our notion of confirmation.

4.2   The Unexpected Examination

The teacher tells the class that sometime during the next week she will give an examination. She will not say on which day for, she says, it is to be a surprise. On the face of it, there is no reason why the teacher, despite having made this announcement, should not be able to do exactly what she has announced: give the class an unexpected examination. It will not be totally unexpected, since the class will know, or at least have good reason to believe, that it will occur sometime during the next week. However, surely it could be a surprise, or unexpected, in this sense: that on the morning of the day on which it is given, the class will have no good reason to believe that it will occur on *that* day, even though they knew, or had good reason to believe, the teacher's announcement. Cannot the teacher achieve this aim by, say, giving the examination on Wednesday?

The class reasons as follows. Let us suppose that the teacher will carry out her threat, in both its parts: that is, she will give an examination, and it will be unexpected. Then the teacher cannot give the examination on Friday (assuming this to be the last possible day of the week); for, by the time Friday morning arrives, and we know that all the previous days have been examination-free, we would have every reason to expect the examination to occur on Friday. So leaving the examination until Friday is inconsistent with giving an *unexpected* examination. For similar reasons, the examination cannot be held on Thursday. Given our previous conclusion that it cannot be delayed until Friday, we would know, when Thursday morning came, and the previous days had been examination-free, that it would have to be held on Thursday. So if it were held on Thursday, it would not be unexpected. Thus it cannot be held on Thursday. Similar reasoning supposedly shows that there is no day of the week on which it can be held, and so supposedly shows that the supposition that the teacher can carry out her threat must be rejected. This is paradoxical, for it seems plain that the teacher *can* carry out her threat.

Something must be wrong with the way in which the class reasoned; but what?

The class's argument falls into two parts: one applies to whether there can be an unexpected examination on the last day, Friday; the other takes forward the negative conclusion on this issue, and purports to extend it to the other days.

Let us begin by looking more closely at the first part. On Friday morning, the possibilities can be divided up as follows:

(a)   The examination will take place on Friday and the class will expect this.

(b)   The examination will take place on Friday and the class will not expect this.

(c)   The examination will not take place on Friday and the class will expect this.

(d)   The examination will not take place on Friday and the class will not expect this.

When we speak of the class's expectations, we mean their rational or well-grounded ones. It is not to the point that they may have expectations to which they are not entitled, or lack expectations to which they are entitled. For example, it is not to the point that the class might irrationally (without entitlement or justification) believe that the examination would take place on Wednesday. Even if it then did take place on Wednesday, this would not show that the teacher's announcement was false, for what she said, as we have interpreted it, was that the class would have *no good reason* to believe that it would occur when it did.

The overall structure of the class's argument is meant to be a *reductio ad absurdum*: they take as a supposition that the teacher's announcement is true, then aim to show that this leads to a contradiction, and hence that the supposition must be rejected. In this first part of the argument, the supposition is used to show that the examination cannot occur on Friday. This is extended to every day of the week in the second part of the argument, so that, in the end, the supposition is rejected. Thus the teacher's announcement is disproved.

Given that the examination has not occurred on the previous days, at most possibility (b) is consistent with the truth of the teacher's announcement. The class's argument aims to show that (b) is not a real possibility.

The idea is that the class can infer that if the examination occurs on Friday, then the announcement is false, contrary to the supposition. The inference is based on the consideration that the class will know that Friday is the last possible day for the examination. So, given the supposition that the teacher's announcement is true, they would expect the examination, were it to occur on Friday; but this is inconsistent with the truth of the announcement. If we hold on to the supposition, the examination cannot take place on Friday.

That this argument is not straightforward can be brought out in the following way. Imagine yourself in the class, and it is Friday morning. There is surely a real question, which you may well feel that you do not know how to answer: has the teacher forgotten or changed her mind, or will the examination indeed take place that day? It would seem that this doubt is enough to ensure that if it does take place that day, it will be unexpected: the class was not entitled to expect it.

The class's argument is meant to circumvent this difficulty by using the truth of the teacher's announcement as a supposition – one that, in the end, is going to be rejected. Given this supposition, the class on Friday morning can rule out the non-occurrence of the examination. On the other hand, it can also rule out its occurrence – and this is what is meant to show that, if the supposition is true, the examination cannot occur on Friday.

However, it is a mistake to think that the supposition merely of the *truth* of the teacher's announcement will do the required work. To see this, imagine ourselves once more among the class on Friday morning. Suppose that the teacher's announcement is true but that we do not know or even believe this. Then we may not believe that the examination will occur. This is enough to make the truth of the announcement possible: if the examination does occur, we shall not have expected it. This shows a fallacy in the reasoning as so far presented. Merely supposing, for *reductio,* that the teacher's announcement is true is not enough to establish that the examination will not be held on Friday. At that point in the argument, we need as a supposition that we *know* that the teacher's announcement is true (Quine 1953).

If we are to have a paradoxical argument worth discussing, we need to make some changes. The details are quite complicated: to make the discussion manageable, we shall soon need to use some abbreviations. Those who dislike symbols might prefer to step off the ride at this point.

4.3   Revising the Unexpected Examination

One modification we could make is to leave the announcement unchanged but alter the structure of the argument. Instead of taking the announcement itself as our supposition, we shall suppose that the class *knows* the truth of the announcement. This supposition is refutable, on Friday, by the considerations outlined. If on Friday we know that the announcement is true, we know that the examination will occur on Friday. If we know that the examination will occur on Friday, the announcement is not true. If the announcement is not true, then we do not know that it is true. The supposition that we know that it is true entails its own falsehood, and so can be rejected. Applying similar reasoning to the other days of the week, the upshot would be that the class can show that it cannot *know* that the announcement is true. This may seem paradoxical: intuitively, we want to say that we knew, from the announcement, that there would be an examination sometime, though we did not know when, and so it was unexpected.

An alternative modification involves changing the announcement to include the fact that the class will not know, on the basis of the announcement, that the examination will take place on the day that it does. In a way that can only be made clear by some abbreviations, this will give us a valid argument for the conclusion that the announcement is false. If this is paradoxical, it is because it seems intuitively obvious that such an announcement could be true.

Let us call the original version of the argument OV, the first proposed modified version MV1, and the second proposed modified version MV2. Since the number of days of the week is irrelevant, let us simplify by supposing that there are just two possible examination days, Monday or Tuesday. For OV and MV1, I shall abbreviate the announcement as:

> **A1**   I shall give you an examination on either Monday or Tuesday, and you will not know – or have good reason to believe – on the morning of the examination that it will occur that day.

The other abbreviations are as follows:

> M for "the examination occurs on Monday";
> T for "the examination occurs on Tuesday";.
> $K_M(...)$ for "the class knows on Monday morning that ..."; and
> $K_T(...)$ for "the class knows on Tuesday morning that ...."

We can express A1 symbolically as:

> $([M$ and not-$K_M(M)]$ or $[T$ and not-$K_T(T)])$ and not both M and T.

(That is, either there will be an examination on Monday and the class does not know this on Monday morning, or there will be an examination on Tuesday and the class does not know this on

Tuesday morning; and there will be an exam on at most one morning.)[8]

OV can be represented as follows:

1. Suppose A1
   2. Suppose not-M
      3. K_T(not-M)   (from 2 + memory)
      4. If not-M, T   (by the definition of A1)
      5. K_T(T)   (from 3 + 4)
      6. If K_T(T) and not-M then not-A1 (by the definition of A1)
      7. not-A1   (from 2, 5, + 6)
   8. M (and so not-T)   (from 1, 2, and 7)
   9. K_M(M)   (from 8 + A1)
  10. If K_M(M) and not-T, then not-A1 (definition of A1)
  11. not-A1   (from 8, 9, + 10)
12. not-A1   (from 1 + 11)

The overall shape of the argument is *reductio ad absurdum*: one makes an assumption in order to show that it leads to a contradiction and so must be rejected. In the present case, the supposition of A1 is supposed to lead eventually to the conclusion that A1 is false. (Indentation is used to show that – and how – some steps of the argument occur within the scope of a supposition. For references and further details see the Bibliographical Notes.) It seems that we intuitively hold that A1 can be true; and that clash constitutes the paradox.

OV suffers from the defect that no adequate justification is provided for step (5). The idea is meant to be this: if A1 is true, then the examination must occur on Tuesday if it does not occur on Monday; so if we knew the examination did not occur on Monday, we would know that it would occur on Tuesday. However, this is not a sound inference: we would also need to *know* that the examination must occur on Tuesday if it does not occur on Monday.[9]

MV1 can be represented as follows:

1. Suppose K(A1)
   2. Suppose not-M
      3. K_T(not-M)   (from 2 + memory)

---

[8] Would it be better to have A1 abbreviate the following?
      (M or T) and not-K_M(M) and not-K_T(T)

[9] Can you give a simple example which brings out why this pattern of inference is not sound? Is the step at line (9) unsound for the same reason? Can the argument be repaired by including an assumption to the effect that the class does know that if the examination does not occur on Monday, then it will occur on Tuesday?

4. If not-M, T	(by definition of A1)
5. K_T(If not-M, T)	(by supposition 1)
6. K_T(T)	(from 3 + 5)
7. If K_T(T), then not-A1	(definition of A1)
8. If not-A1, then not-K(A1)	(only truth is known)
9. If K_T(T) then not-K(A1)	(from 7 + 8)
10. M (and so not-T)	(from 1,6 and 9)
11. K_M(M)	(from 10)[10]
12. If K_M(M) and M, then not-A1	(definition of A1)
13. not-A1	(from 10, 11, + 12)
14. If not-A1, then not-K(A1)	(only truth is known)
15. not-K(A1)	(from 13 + 14)
16. not-K(A1)	(from 1 + 15)

Even if MV1 is valid (and question 10 below gives a reason for doubt on this point), it is questionable whether there is anything paradoxical in this conclusion. To have a paradox, we would need also to have an argument for the conclusion that K(A1). Perhaps it is just intuitively obvious that K(A1), given, if you like, the class's knowledge of the teacher's unimpeachable reputation for veracity and constancy of purpose; but suppose someone failed to share this intuition?

If not-K(A1), then it is very easy for A1 to be true: the class will not on the basis of A1 have any expectations, since the students can establish that they cannot know A1. This gives the teacher plenty of scope for surprising them.

However, the class can also go through the reasoning of the preceding paragraph: "Our proof that A1 cannot be known shows us how easy it is for A1 to be true. If it *can* be true, then, given the teacher's proven veracity and determination, we have every reason to believe that it *is* true". If the class is led by this consideration to believe the announcement, then there is a case for thinking that

---

10 The argument is suspect at this point. We have supposedly proved M [at (10)] on the basis of K(A1). It is quite plausible to hold that this means that we can know the corresponding conditional, viz.:

If K(A1), then M.

To obtain K_M(M) from K[If K(A1), then M] would appear to require as a premise not merely K(A1), but K[K(A1)]. We should avoid obtaining the latter by the dubious principle:

If K(φ), then K[K(φ)].

Why is this principle dubious? Might the argument manage with something weaker?

their belief amounts to knowledge. So it seems that *if* the argument is valid, we have a paradox.[11]

MV2 requires a different announcement:

A2   Either [M and not-K_M (If A2, then M)] or [T and not-K_T (If A2, then T)].

(That is, the examination will take place on Monday or Tuesday, but you will not know on the basis of this announcement which day it will be.) A2 differs from A1 in a striking respect: the specification of A2 refers to A2 itself; in other words, A2 is a *self-referential* announcement.

MV2 can be represented as follows:

1. Suppose A2
    2. Suppose not-M
        3. K_T(not-M)   (from 2 + memory)
        4. K_T(If not-M, then if A2, then   (the class understands
           T)   A2)
        5. K_T(If A2, then T)   (from 3 + 4)
        6. not-A2   (from 2 + 5)
    7. M   (from 1, 2 + 6)
    8. If A2, then M   (summarizing 1–7)
    9. K_M(If A2, then M)   (the proved is known)
    10. If K_M(If A2, then M), then if A2,   (from definition of A2)
        then not-M
    11. If A2, then not-M   (from 9 + 10)
12. not-A2   (from 8 + 11)

MV2 purports to prove that A2 is not true. This is paradoxical only if we have some good reason to think that A2 is, or could be, true. We seem to have some reason: have we not all been exposed to such threats of unexpected examinations? The form of A2 admit-

---

[11] Once one starts thinking about knowledge, one can rather easily convince oneself that there is less of it than one might have thought. So I would not be surprised if someone were to say "We could not *know* that the teacher would carry out her threat, however reliable we knew her to have been in the past. The most we would be entitled to is the justified belief that she would."

Rework MV1 in terms of justified belief rather than knowledge. (You will probably find you have to make an inference from "It was rational for the class to believe the teacher's announcement when it was made" to "It would be rational for the class to believe the teacher's announcement on the morning of the last day, if the exam had not yet been given". Is this inference sound? Is the parallel inference in the case of knowledge sound? At what points was it assumed in the arguments displayed above?)

tedly has the self-referential feature already noticed, but it is not clear that this should detract from its possible truth. When the teacher says that the examination is to be unexpected, what is clearly intended is that it be unexpected on any basis, including on the basis of this present announcement. So the intuitions that told us that A1 could be true, and could be known, should also tell us that A2 could be true. However, intuition may be less than wholly confident when faced with the apparent validity of MV2.

4.4   The Knower

Using a self-referential type of announcement, one can construct a further announcement, call it A3, that is certainly paradoxical. It has come to be called the Knower paradox:

> **A3**   K(not-A3).

(As we might put it: "The class knows that this very announcement is false".)

We can represent the argument that establishes both A3 and not-A3 as follows – call it MV3:

1. Suppose A3	
2. K(not-A3)	(definition of A3)
3. not-A3	(what is known is true)
4. If A3, then not-A3	(summarizing 1–3)
5. not-A3	(from 4)
6. not-K(not-A3)	(from 5 + definition of A3)
7. K(not-A3)	(5 + what is proved is known)

Lines (6) and (7) are contradictory.

In view of this result, we must examine carefully (a) the nature of the announcement and (b) the epistemic principles – the principles involving the nature of knowledge – used to reach the paradoxical conclusion. If there is anything wrong with the principles, then we may have to revise our views about the earlier arguments, for they, too, rest on these principles.

(a)   We cannot satisfy ourselves merely by saying that A3 is contradictory. A contradiction is false, whereas A3, if the argument MV3 is sound, is demonstrably true (see line 7). More hopeful would be to say that A3 is *unintelligible,* perhaps in part because of its self-referentiality. What, we might ask, does it *say*? What is it that it claims cannot be known? If we say it claims that it itself cannot be known, we seem to be grappling in thin air rather than genuinely answering the question.

Some of this doubt might be removed by changing the example. Suppose now that we have two teachers, X and Y. X says "What Y will say next is something you can know to be false". Y then says "What X has just said is true". It looks as though we have to count both utterances as intelligible, since in other contexts they certainly would have been intelligible, and even in this context we can understand X's without knowing what Y will say, and can understand Y's without knowing what X has said. However, in the context Y's announcement appears to be equivalent to A3. We could argue informally for the contradiction like this. Suppose Y is true (let X and Y now also abbreviate the respective teachers' remarks). Then X is true, so you can know Y to be false, so it is false. So the supposition that Y is true leads to the conclusion that it is false. Hence we can conclude that it is false (cf. MV3, line 5). Hence we can conclude that *we can know Y to be false*. However, if Y is false, then X is false; i.e., *we cannot know Y to be false*. So it seems we have an argument that has the essential features of A3, but which has a defence against the charge that the announcement is unintelligible. (Compare Burge 1978, p. 30.)

(b)   Let us isolate the three epistemic principles concerning knowledge appealed to in MV3. The first – call it EK1 – is what licenses the move from (2) to (3) in MV3. In its most general form it is that what is known is true. We could write it:

EK1   If $K(\varphi)$, then φ.

The other point at which appeal to epistemic principles is made is the move at (7) from (5). It cannot be true that anything that is provable on the basis of no matter what assumptions is knowable. Given as assumption that $5 > 7$, I could perhaps prove that $5 > 6$ on that assumption, but obviously I could not *know* that $5 > 6$. So the principle that we need at this point is that anything proved from known assumptions (or from no assumptions) is known.[12] We could write this as:

EK2   If C is provable from $(P_1, ..., P_n)$ and $K(P_1, ..., P_n)$, then $K(C)$.

What assumptions (corresponding to P_1, etc.) are in play in the move from (5) to (7)? Just one: EK1. So, in order to apply EK2, we need to add:

---

[12] Compare with the principle sometimes called "epistemic closure":
    If K(if φ, then ψ) and $K(\varphi)$, then $K(\psi)$.
   Is EK2 entailed by the closure principle? Does the converse entailment hold?

EK3   K(EK1).

Are these three principles plausible? Expressed informally they are the following:

EK1   What is known is true.
EK2   What is provable from things known is known.
EK3   It is known that what is known is true.

The first principle has sometimes been doubted on the grounds that, for example, people once knew that whales were fish; but this doubt is dispelled by the reflection that the correct account of the matter is that people *thought* they knew this, although they really did not. How could they have known it if it is not even true?

EK2 does not hold generally: we do not know all the infinitely many things that could be proved from what we know; we do not even believe all these things, if only because it would be beyond our powers to bring them all to mind. However, this implausible aspect of EK2 is not required for the paradox, which only needs a much narrower claim: that at least one person who has constructed a correct proof of not-A3 from a known premise knows that not-A3.

The third principle cannot be seriously questioned, once we have granted the first. So the only doubt about the premises attaches to EK2. We could circumvent this by using an even weaker and very hard to controvert principle: what is provable from something known is *capable* of being known by a fully rational subject. With appropriate modifications to A3, we shall be able to prove a contradiction from principles that appear indubitable, together with the admission of the intelligibility of the teacher's announcement.[13]

It is hard to know what to make of this paradox. One promising suggestion sees a similarity between it and the Liar paradox (see sections 5.2ff below). Knowledge quite clearly involves the notion of truth, and the Liar paradox shows that this notion can lead to paradox. So perhaps what is at fault in the concept of knowledge is the concept of truth it contains, as displayed in EK1; and perhaps the remedy consists in applying to knowledge whatever non-paradoxical elaboration of the notion of truth we can extract from consideration of the Liar paradox.

The suggestion cannot be quite right for the following reason. Unlike knowledge, belief does not entail truth; yet a paradox rather

---

[13]   Provide the modified A3 (call it A4) and the appropriate argument, setting out the epistemic principles in detail.

like the Knower – we could call it the Believer – can be constructed in terms just of belief. Consider the following:

> **B₁**   α does not believe what B₁ says.[14]

Does α believe B₁ or not? If α does believe B₁, then he can see that he is believing something false. There is no gap between seeing that something is false and not believing it, so if α believes B₁, he does not believe it. Equally, if α does not believe B₁, then he can see that B₁ is true. There is no gap between seeing that something is true and believing it, so if α does not believe B₁, he believes it.

The paradox depends on at least two assumptions:

> (1)   that α *can* see that, if he believes B₁, it is false, and if he does not believe it, it is true;
>
> (2)   that what α can see he *will* see.

Neither assumption would be capable of true generalization. For (1) to hold of α requires, among other things, that he be able to see that he is α. One could arguably envisage this not being true, if α had an unusually low level of self-awareness. For (2) to hold of α requires a positive level of intellectual energy: one does not always take advantage of one's epistemic opportunities. However, we have a paradox if we can make the following highly plausible assumption: that there is at least one person with the self-awareness and energy required to make (1) and (2) true of him (or her), at least in respect of B₁.

We can represent the argument to the contradiction, and the assumptions upon which it depends, in a manner analogous to the representation of the Knower paradox. (For a different version, see Burge 1978, esp. p. 26.) We abbreviate "α believes that ( )" as "B( )"; so $B_1 = \text{not-}B(B_1)$.

1. Suppose $B(B_1)$
2. If $B(B_1)$, then $B[B(B_1)]$ (self-awareness)
3. $B[B(B_1)]$ (from 1 + 2)
4. $B[\text{If } B_1, \text{ then not-}B(B_1)]$ (α understands B₁)
5.   If $B[B(B_1)]$, then not-$B[\text{not-}B(B_1)]$ (rationality)
6.   not-$B[\text{not-}B(B_1)]$ (from 3 + 5)
7.   not-$B(B_1)$ (4, 6, + closure)
8. If $B(B_1)$, then not-$B(B_1)$ (summarizing 1–7)

---

[14] Construct a version of the Believer analogous to the "What I am now saying is false" version of the Liar.

9. not-$B(B_1)$ (from 8)
10. $B[\text{not-}B(B_1)]$ (from 9 + self-awareness)
11. $B(B_1)$ (from 10 + definition of B_1)

The unconditionally derived lines (9) and (11) are contradictory.

Let us examine the assumptions upon which the argument depends. The first principle to be used is what I have called "self-awareness". In its most general form it could be represented as follows:

EB1   If $B(\varphi)$, then $B[B(\varphi)]$.

This is not very plausible. If it were true, then having one belief, say φ, would involve having infinitely many: that you believe that φ, that you believe you believe that φ, and so on. However, all that is required for the paradox are two instances of EB1: that if α believes B_1, under circumstances that can be as favourable as you like to self-awareness, then he will believe he does so; and if α does not believe B_1, then he will believe he does not. It seems impossible to deny that there could be a person of whom this is true.

The second assumption is that α understands B_1 and therefore realizes (and so believes), from the definition of B_1, that if B_1, then not-$B(B_1)$. Again, it seems impossible to deny that there could be a person who has this belief.

Next comes the principle called rationality. A generalization would be the following:

EB2   If $B(\varphi)$ then not-$B(\text{not-}\varphi)$.

Put so generally, this is not plausible, since people in fact have contradictory beliefs without realizing it; but we need only impute a fairly modest degree of rationality to α in order for the weakest premise needed at line (5) to obtain.

A generalization of the closure principle is this:

EB3   If $B(\text{if } \varphi, \text{ then } \psi)$ and $B(\text{not-}\psi)$, then $B(\text{not-}\varphi)$.

For normal persons, this is not a plausible principle: we do not believe all the consequences of things we believe. However, it again seems easy to imagine that α verifies the particular case of the principle needed in the above argument.

Let us step back. A suggestion was that the Knower paradox should be treated like the Liar paradox, on the grounds that knowledge entails truth, and the Liar paradox shows that the notion of truth requires special treatment. The point of introducing the Believer paradox was to challenge this suggestion. Belief does not entail truth, yet belief gives rise to a paradox quite similar to the Knower.

The conclusion is that the reason given for treating the Knower and the Liar in similar ways is deficient. However, there is another similarity between the Knower, the Believer and the Liar: they all involve self-reference, as does any version of the Unexpected Examination which (like MV2) involves a self-referential announcement. We shall see in sections 5.6–5.8 below that there is a case for thinking that some kinds of self-reference prevent apparently intelligible utterances from being genuinely intelligible. If the case is good, it should be considered as the basis of a possible response to the Knower, the Believer, and self-referential versions of the Unexpected Examination.

Bibliographical notes

Section 4.1.1
David Hume assumed that it was easy to answer the problem of characterization in the way envisaged in this section: the arguments we take to be legitimate are those in which it is assumed that the future will resemble the past. This suggestion is shown to be inadequate by the Grue paradox. Hume (1738, Book I, Part III) remains essential reading on the problem of the justification of induction, and on various connected issues, notably causation. A good introduction and overview is Skyrms (1975).

Section 4.1.2
Hempel (1945) gives a classic account of the paradox of the Ravens. I have departed from Hempel's formulation of E2. The equivalence relation he uses is that of *logical* equivalence, not *a priori* equivalence. Two propositions are logically equivalent just on condition that some system of formal logic has a theorem saying that either both propositions are true, or else both are false. Thus "Tom is a bachelor" and "Tom is a bachelor or the earth is round or not-round" are logically equivalent, but "Tom is a bachelor" and "Tom is an unmarried man" are not logically equivalent (though they can be known *a priori* to be equivalent). The intuitive motivation for the equivalence principle is this, in my view: if P and Q are in the appropriate sense equivalent, then if we can find evidence supporting P, we need no further empirical data to see that Q is thereby supported to the same extent. If this motivation is accepted, it seems clear that the appropriate equivalence relation is wider than logical equivalence, and is, precisely, *a priori* equivalence.

For a brief introduction to confirmation theory, see Schlesinger (1974a). A useful collection of early papers is in Foster and Martin (1966).

Section 4.1.3

The classic source of the Grue paradox is Goodman (1955). There has been controversy about how Goodman defines "grue". He writes that "grue" is to be introduced so that:

> it applies to all things examined before *t* just in case they are green but to other things just in case they are blue. (1955, p. 74)

The time *t* is arbitrary. In giving my account, I have imagined ourselves being at that time: if all emeralds are now grue, the examined ones are now green and the unexamined ones blue; there is no question of an emerald having to change colour to stay grue. For discussion of some alternative interpretations, see Jackson (1975).

My G2-4 were inspired by Jackson, whose own proposal is:

> certain *F*s which are *H* being *G* does not support other *F*s which are not *H* being *G* if it is known that the *F*s in the evidence class would not have been *G* if they had not been *H* (Jackson 1975, p. 123).

These proposals contain a subjunctive conditional ("If it had not been that ..., it would not have been that ..."), and so would not be acceptable to Goodman, whose overall project is to give an account of such conditionals. However, there is nothing in the nature of the characterization problem as such (section 4.1.1) which precludes the use of subjunctive conditionals in its solution.

The view that instances alone cannot make it reasonable to believe a generalization has been advocated by Foster (1983).

The example of "+*" derives from Wittgenstein (1953), esp. pp.□185ff, and has been revived by Kripke (1982). Goodman's own philosophical development has been influenced by what he would regard as ramifications of the Grue paradox – see Goodman (1978, p. 11).

Section 4.2

The paradox goes back at least to Scriven (1951); a good early discussion is Quine (1953). Recent work includes Bar-Hillel and Margalit (1983), (1985), Janaway (1989), Koons (1992) and Williamson (1992a). See also "The Grid" and "The Designated Student" in Appendix I of the present volume, and compare Sorensen (1982).

G. E. Moore considered that it was paradoxical for me to assert "*p,* but I do not believe that *p,*" despite the fact that the quoted sentence is consistent and, indeed, the fact it expresses might be true of me. (E.g., you could truly say of me: "*p,* but he does not believe it".) This may be connected with the Unexpected Examination: see Wright and Sudbury (1977).

Section 4.3

The proofs are set out in a style invented by Fitch (1952). The style is used in several more recent books, e.g. Thomason (1970). I hope that their intended structure will be self-explanatory, but some observations may be useful.

For example, what is the difference between lines (7), (11), and (12) on p. 95? Each has the same conclusion, but it has been reached from different suppositions, as the different degrees of indentation show. At (7), the argument claims that we have reached not-A1 on the basis of supposing that A1 is true and that not-M is true. This would mean that we have reached a contradiction: since anything entails itself, the supposition of both A1 and not-M leads to the contradiction that A1 and not-A1. We must therefore reject at least one of these. Line (8) claims that if we hold on to A1, we must reject not-M (equivalently, T). At line (11), not-A1 depends only on the supposition of A1 itself. In other words, at this point we have shown that A1 entails its own negation. This is enough to show that, on the basis of *no* suppositions at all, we can infer the falsehood of A1, since anything entailing its own negation is false, and this is what (12), by having *no* indent, expresses.

Section 4.4

The classic statement of the Knower is Montague and Kaplan (1960). A similar paradox is in Buridan's Sophism 13; see Hughes (1982). For the Believer, and a comparison with the Liar, see Burge (1984). I offer no view about whether believing or knowing are to be properly represented by an operator or by a predicate. Those who prefer the operator treatment will have to read "A1", as it occurs in the formal argument, as short for "A1 is true". Those who prefer the predicate treatment will have to read various expressions within the scope of K as names of (equiform) expressions, rather than as expressions in use. Montague and Kaplan (1960) present the paradox using the predicate treatment to avert the suspicion that operators are to blame (see p. 272). Nicholas Asher and Hans Kamp (personal commununication) take the Knower paradox to bear essentially on the question of what is the appropriate account of propositional attitude constructions.

5.   Classes and truth

The paradoxes to be discussed in this chapter are probably the hardest of all, but also the most fecund. Russell's paradox about classes, which he discovered in 1901, led to an enormous amount of work in the foundations of mathematics. Russell thought that this paradox was of a kind with the paradox of the Liar, which in its simplest form consists in the assertion "I am now (hereby!) lying". The Liar paradox has been of the utmost importance in theories of truth. Everything to do with these paradoxes is highly controversial, including whether Russell was right in thinking that his paradox about classes and the Liar paradox spring from the same source (see section 5.9).

5.1   Russell's paradox

If Socrates is a man, then he is a member of the class of men. If he is a member of the class of men, then he is a man. Can *classes* be members of classes? The answer would seem to be Yes. The class of men has more than 100 members, so the class of men is a member of the class of classes with more than 100 members. By contrast, the class of the Muses does not belong to the class of classes having more than 100 members, for tradition has it that the class of Muses has just nine members.

Most classes are not members of themselves. The class of men is a class and not a man, so it is not a member of the class of men, that is, not a member of itself. However, some classes are members of themselves: the class of all classes presumably is, and so is the class of all classes with more than 100 members. So is the class of non-men: the class of all and only those things that are not men. No class is a man, so the class of non-men is not a man, and is therefore a member of the class of non-men.

Consider the class of all classes that are not members of themselves. Let us call this class R. The necessary and sufficient condition for something to belong to R is that it be a class that is not a member of itself. Is R a member of itself?

Suppose that it is. Then R must meet the (necessary) condition for belonging to R: that it is not a member of itself. So if it is a member of itself, it is not a member of itself.

Suppose that it is not. Then, being a non-self-membered class, it meets the (sufficient) condition for belonging to R: that it is not a member of itself. So if it is not a member of itself, it belongs to R, and so is a member of itself.

Summarizing: R is a member of itself if and only if it is not a member of itself. This is contradictory.[1]

To have a contradiction is not necessarily to have a paradox. Recall the Barber paradox from the Introduction. The barber shaves all and only those who do not shave themselves. Who shaves the barber? By reasoning similar to that used to derive Russell's paradox, we find that the barber shaves himself if and only if he does not.

We respond to the Barber paradox simply by saying that there is no such barber. Why should we not respond to Russell's paradox simply by saying that there is no such class as R? The difference is this: nothing leads us to suppose that there is such a barber; but we seem to be committed, by our understanding of what it is to be a class, to the existence of R. We are forced by the paradox to accept that there cannot be such a class. This is paradoxical because it shows that some very compelling views about what it is for a class to exist have to be abandoned.

The first paragraph of this section was supposed to introduce the natural or intuitive view of classes, which I must now make more explicit. I said that if Socrates *is a man,* then he is a member of the class of men. Let us use "condition" for what is expressed by, for example, the italicized phrase just used. Being a man is a condition, and one that Socrates satisfies, although Mont Blanc does not. The natural view of classes includes this principle of Class Existence:

Handwritten margin notes (left): The class of men is men / no class of men is < class / if s < class / not a man / of ... on a class of men, not a man. So how / does not can't apply to itself / How can class of men be part of class of men?

Handwritten note (bottom center): The class of classes is a class of itself - or classes

---

[1] The Class paradox, as Russell saw, is very similar to one about properties. Most properties are not applicable to themselves. The property of being a man is a property and not a man, so it does not apply to the property of being a man; that is, it is not self-applicable. However, some properties are self-applicable: the property of being a property presumably is, and so is the property of being a property true of more than 100 things; etc.
How would you spell out the contradiction?

CE   To every intelligible condition there corresponds a class: its members (if any) are all and only the things that satisfy the condition.

Corresponding to the condition of being a man, there is the class of men. Even when a condition is contradictory – for example, the condition of being both square and not square – there corresponds a class; though since nothing meets the condition, this is a class with no members (the empty or "null" class).

CE appears to lead to Russell's paradox. It entails that there is such a class as R if there is the intelligible condition: being a class that is not a member of itself. The condition appears intelligible; yet we have already seen that there cannot be such a class as R.

We could put this point in a more symbolic and more perspicuous way as follows. Let us use "ε" to abbreviate "is a member of" (and "belongs to"). Then we can rewrite CE as follows:

CE   For every intelligible condition F, there is a class x, such that: for anything y, $y \, \varepsilon x$ if and only if y satisfies F.

For "y satisfies F" we can write, simply, "y is F"; for "if and only if" we can write "iff". Putting "R" for Russell's paradoxical class, "$\neg$" for "not", and "$\neg$ a member of itself" for F, CE yields:

For anything y, $y \, \varepsilon \, R$ iff $\neg$ (y is a member of itself).

For something, y, to be a member of itself is presumably for it to belong to y, so we can rewrite the above as:

For anything y , $y \, \varepsilon \, R$ iff $\neg$ ($y \, \varepsilon y$).

What holds for anything must hold for R, so we get the explicitly contradictory:

RP $R \, \varepsilon \, R$ iff $\neg$ ($R \, \varepsilon R$).

A natural suggestion is that the condition "being non-self-membered" is not genuinely intelligible – and this is, in effect, what most responses to Russell's paradox propose. If we follow this suggestion, CE can be preserved, as long as we take a sufficiently narrow view about what constitutes a condition. However, if we are also to preserve some well-known results in mathematics, it is far from obvious what this narrower view ought to be. In particular, reasoning and assumptions very like those that occur in the derivation of Russell's paradox also occur in a famous proof by Cantor, which I shall now set out. Indeed, it was studying

Cantor's proof that led Russell to the discovery of the paradox. It is hard to see how to block the paradox while allowing the proof.

What is to be proved is that the power class of any class has more members than the class. (For a definition of power class, see the Bibliographical Notes.) Cantor's proof could be sketched informally as follows:

1. A class must have *at least* as many subclasses as members, since for each member the unit class to which it alone belongs is a subclass.

2. So either there are as many subclasses as members or more.

3. Suppose there are as many. This means that there is a one–one function f correlating members of the class with its subclasses.

4. Now form the following subclass S: $x \, \varepsilon \, S$ iff $\neg \, [x \, \varepsilon \, f(x)]$. By the supposition at (3), for some α, $S = f(\alpha)$. Applying the definition of S we get:
    $\alpha \, \varepsilon \, S$ iff $\neg \, [\alpha \, \varepsilon f(\alpha)]$

Therefore, given $S = f(\alpha)$:

(*) $\alpha \, \varepsilon \, S$ iff $\neg \, (\alpha \, \varepsilon S)$.

5. This contradiction shows that we must reject the supposition at (3). Hence we must adopt the other alternative available in (2): a class has more subclasses than members.

In (4) we have a contradiction which resembles that involved in Russell's paradox (compare the asterisked line with RP), but here used to serious and informative effect in the proof. The proof assumes that *if* there is a function f, then there is a subclass S. If we are to use the current suggestion that an over liberal interpretation of CE is to blame for the paradox, and yet preserve Cantor's proof, we need to find a restriction on the notion of a *condition* that allows, via CE, the hypothetical existence of the class S but disallows the existence of R. Moreover, to be philosophically satisfying, there must be a philosophical justification for the restriction, enabling us to understand the origin of the paradox and to feel that we have something better than an ad hoc blocking manoeuvre. It is to Russell's credit that he attempted to provide precisely this in his Vicious Circle Principle (VCP). His idea is that the condition involved in the specification of R is viciously circular, and therefore not intelligible. He thought that the VCP also explained away a number of other paradoxes including, most important, the Liar paradox. I shall discuss the VCP (in sections 5.8 and 5.9) in the course of the discussion of the Liar (beginning in section 5.2).

For Russell, the VCP provided the philosophical motivation for his Theory of Types, according to which classes are arranged in a hierarchy, in such a way that every class is on a higher level than any of its members. The theory ensures that no class belongs to itself: no expression of the form $x \, \varepsilon x$ counts as meaningful. Simplified versions of Russell's Theory of Types have been the dominant tradition in mathematical work on classes. However, one must distinguish between the Theory of Types on the one hand, a device designed to ensure that paradoxes do not inhibit mathematical work, and, on the other hand, a justification for such a theory, like that which, according to Russell, is provided by the VCP. The justification ought to help us understand what it is about classes which calls for a Theory of Types. The search for understanding of this kind is a distinctively philosophical project, upon which the working mathematician can reasonably decline to engage.

5.2 The Liar: semantic defects

The material of the next four sections is hazardous. (Recall the fate of Philetas, mentioned in the Introduction.)

A relatively recent version of the Liar paradox appears in St Paul's epistle to Titus (1, xii–xiii).[2] This version involves the island of Crete and the notion of lying, and lying involves an intention to deceive. These features are irrelevant to the paradox. Eliminating such irrelevancies, we get something like this:

What I am now saying is false.

The simplest version of all, which will be the starting point of the discussion, is

L_1 L_1 is false.

---

[2] It is not clear that the saint sees any logical, as opposed to moral, problems. The relevant text is as follows:
> 12. One of themselves, even a prophet of their own, said, The Cretans are always liars, evil beasts, slow bellies.
> 13. This witness is true. Wherefore rebuke them sharply, that they may be sound in the faith.

St Paul's version depends on the assumption that all the other Cretans are liars. Construct an explicit argument for the contradiction (perhaps modelled on that given below for L_1) that makes this dependence plain.

Here we have a sentence, called L_1, that is supposed to say of it-self that it is false. One can derive something apparently paradox-ical as follows. Suppose it is true; then it is as it says it is – false. So it is false. However, suppose that it is false. Well, *false* is just what it says it is, and a sentence that tells it the way it is is true. So it is true. To sum up: if L_1 is true, it is false; and if it is false, it is true.

Is this paradoxical? Perhaps it sounds as if it is, but let us look more carefully. We have two conditional claims:

(a)   If L_1 is true, then it is false.
(b)   If L_1 is false, then it is true.

We assume that anything that is false is not true, and anything that is true is not false; so (a) and (b) yield:

(a′)   If L_1 is true, then it is not true.
(b′)   If L_1 is false, then it is not false.

If a sentence implies its own negation, then we can infer that negation. (This principle is called *consequentia mirabilis*. It amounts to the validity of the sequent: $A \rightarrow \neg A \models \neg A$.) Both (a′) and (b′) offer inputs to this principle. The first assures us that "L_1 is true" implies its negation, so the principle tells us that we can infer that L_1 is not true. The second, in an exactly parallel way, enables us to infer that L_1 is not false. So standard reasoning guarantees that L_1 is not true and is also not false. Let us summa-rize this as follows:

G L_1 is neither true nor false.

Is *this* paradoxical? Not unless we have some independent rea-son to suppose that L_1 is either true or false. For example, we might be able to justify some *principle of bivalence*, perhaps to the effect that *every* sentence, and so in particular L_1, is either true or false. Otherwise we might simply *accept* G, saying that L_1 lies in a *gap* between truth and falsehood (hence the "G"). This would not in itself offer a complete account of the paradox, for it would remain to discover general principles to explain why L_1 should fail to be true and fail to be false. But accepting G would at least fix the general approach.

We could not accept G if there were some irresistible reason for supposing that L_1 had to be either true or false. Might there be an irresistible reason for accepting some principle of bivalence? The version given in the preceding paragraph is certainly not true. Questions are expressed in sentences, but no question is either true or false. Suppose then we restrict the principle to declarative, indicative sentences. Still, there are putative counterexamples, for example:

You have stopped beating your wife.

If you have never beaten your wife, the sentence is certainly not true; but to say it is false, or to say that you have not stopped beating your wife, arguably suggests that you are still beating her. Again, consider a case in which someone says

That elephant is about to charge

when there is no elephant in the offing. We certainly cannot count the sentence as true; but can we count it as false? If we did this, should not the following sentence be true?

That elephant is *not* about to charge.

Yet, if there is no elephant, this seems as poor a candidate for truth as the previous one.

Despite the apparent counterexamples, it is hard not to feel the pull of the thought that some principle of bivalence, no doubt suitably refined, ought to be correct. The underlying idea might be expressed like this: any non-defective representation of how things are in the world must be either accurate or inaccurate, true or false. Some sentences, like questions and commands, are not designed to represent the world, so there is no question of them representing it correctly or incorrectly. Other sentences, though designed to represent the world, fail to count as representations at all, correct or incorrect, in virtue of some semantic defect. The case of the missing elephant is a putative example. For that sentence to represent the world at all, it must refer to an elephant (or so it is plausible to suppose). Since it fails to refer, it counts as semantically defective, and so counts as neither true nor false.

In sum, the most natural and immediate response to the Liar is to accept the reasoning which leads to the conclusion that the paradoxical sentence, L_1, is neither true nor false.[3] Since it is hard to suppose that a semantically non-defective sentence could fail to be either true or false, this approach carries with it the obligation to explain wherein the defectiveness of L_1 consists. It would be totally unexplanatory to say that the defect consists in the sentence's potential for paradox, for that potential is precisely what we need to understand.

[3*] Show how the principles of reasoning in this section can apparently be used to derive that L_1 is both true and false. This derivation shows that one could not regard L_1 as a basis for a straightforward proof of G.

Most accounts of the Liar paradox endeavour to establish plausible general principles upon which the Liar sentences are defective. We will consider some of these in detail in subsequent sections.

5.3   Grounding and truth

One approach to identifying a semantic defect in L_1 starts from the idea that the truth of a sentence must be grounded in something outside the sentence itself. We can make the thought vivid by imagining how one might introduce someone to the notion of truth.

We take the learner to understand most of English, but not the word "true". We could try to explain the notion of truth using the following recipe:

> You should call a sentence true iff you are willing to assert it.

("Iff" abbreviates "if and only if".) The learner could use this explanation to respond to, for example, "Snow is white" by saying "True!", and to respond to "Grass is red" by saying "Not true!". However, he could not in the first instance use the explanation to find out how to respond to a sentence like:

> (1)   "Snow is white" is true.

Until he has already understood "true", he cannot know what it would be to be willing to use this sentence to assert something. At a later stage, once he becomes aware that he is to respond with "True!" to "Snow is white", he will be able to see that he should assent to (1), and hence see that (1) is itself something to which "true" applies. The picture is of someone climbing a ladder. At the base there are sentences not containing the word "true", to which he can learn to apply the word. As he does so, he can thereby come to see how to apply the word to sentences such as (1) on the next rung up; sentences applying "true" to sentences at the base. He can work his way up this ladder indefinitely. Where S is a sentence not containing "true", he can use this process to understand any sentence of the form

> ... "S is true" ... is true,

where the second ellipsis stands in for any number of further occurrences of "is true".[4]

---

4   What does the first ellipsis indicate?

Learning how to apply the concept of truth requires there to be sentences that do not themselves invoke this concept: the *base* sentences. The learning situation mirrors a putative metaphysical fact: that *truth depends on something outside itself.* One might defend the claim that L_1 is neither true nor false on the grounds that L_1 does not respect this fact. Accordingly, it is semantically defective. Let me try to explain this.

Whether or not "Snow is white" is true depends on whether or not snow is white. In this simple case, whether or not something is true depends quite directly on a fact that can be expressed without invoking the concept of truth: on whether or not snow is white. This is an example of what I mean by saying that truth depends upon something outside itself. In more complex cases, the dependence is less direct. For example, consider (1) again ("Snow is white" is true). Whether (1) is true depends on whether or not "Snow is white" is true. This in turn depends on whether or not snow is white. So whether or not (1) is true depends, but at one remove, on whether or not snow is white. In the end, we get back to a non-truth-involving question. In this reflection, we travel down the ladder toward the base. In considering learning, we were travelling upward from the base – same ladder, different direction.

To reinforce the suggestion, consider this series of sentences:

(S2)   (S1) is true.
(S3)   (S2) is true.
(S4)   (S3) is true.
              ...

Can we genuinely make sense of such a series? Everything depends upon what (S1) is. If it is, for example, "Snow is white", then there is no problem: we reach base. However, we would never reach base if (S1) were, for example,

(S1)   (S4) is true.

Here truth wanders in a circle, without ever touching the ground. In this case we need to say that none of the sentences is true – and also, for the same reason, none is false (Kripke 1975).

This line of thinking gives a general reason for accepting G (L_1 is neither true nor false). L_1 can never reach base: there is no getting to a non-truth-involving fact on which the truth or falsehood of L_1 could depend. We come back always to L_1 itself, which is not a base sentence. To summarize: the trouble with L_1 is that it is *ungrounded.*

The same account also applies well to

T₁ T_1 is true.

Here is a sentence that seems to say of itself that it is true. It is not paradoxical. The supposition that it is true does not lead to the conclusion that it is not; the supposition that it is not true does not lead to the conclusion that it is. Still, intuitively there is something wrong with T_1, and L_1 shares the defect. The account just given purports to identify this defect: T_1 is ungrounded. Like L_1, it does not make contact with a non-truth-involving base, so both sentences are neither true nor false.

Thus G can be defended. We can provide reasons, independently of threat of paradox, for thinking that L_1 is neither true nor false: it is ungrounded. But even if all this is accepted, paradox remains.

5.4   The Strengthened Liar

G says that L_1 is neither true nor false, and thus accepts the reasoning we considered at the beginning of section 5.2. However, G itself appears to support a paradox.

G entails that L_1 is not false. But this is the negation of L_1 itself. So G entails

not-L₁ L_1 is not false.

So not-L_1 is true (using the principle that anything which entails a sentence entails the truth of that sentence). This in turn entails that L_1 is false (using the principle that any sentence whose negation is true is false). So G appears to entail a contradiction: that L_1 is not false and L_1 is false.[5] Hence it cannot constitute a resolution of the paradox.

A related difficulty is that G is unable to deal with a related paradoxical sentence:

L_G L_G is either false, or else neither true nor false.

We can reason as follows: suppose L_G is neither true nor false; then it is true (since an or-statement is true if one of its alternatives is), and so it is either true or false. We can then reason as we did with L_1 to show that it is neither true nor false. Combining results, we show that it is both neither true nor false, and also either true or false.

[5*] Show how one can (apparently) *derive* that L_1 is not false without appeal to G.

The easiest way to see what is going on in reasoning of this sort is to consider yet another paradoxical sentence:

L$_2$ L$_2$ is not true.

Suppose L$_2$ is true. Then it is as it says it is, viz., not true; so it is not true. Suppose that it is not true. Well, *not true* is just what it says it is, and a sentence that tells it the way it is is true; so it is true. To sum up: if L$_2$ is true, it is not true; if it is not true, it is true.

This appears to be a genuine contradiction, and one which cannot be assuaged by G. If L$_2$ is, as G affirms, neither true nor false, then in particular it is not true. But the reasoning just advanced purports to show that one can refute this claim: if L$_2$ is not true, then it is true (since *not true* is just what it says itself to be).

Nor could we modify G to some view like

G′   L$_2$ is neither true nor not true.

First, this appears to be a contradiction. Standard reasoning would enable us to infer from G′ that L$_2$ is both true *and* not true.[6] Second, like G, G′ implies directly that L$_2$ is not true: it entails the paradoxical sentence itself.

L$_2$ and the attendant reasoning is sometimes known as the "Strengthened Liar". A standard view is that it shows the inadequacy of theories like the one based on the notion of grounding as resolutions of Liar paradoxes. More generally, it might be taken to show that any approach which tries to resolve the paradox by finding some semantic defect in L$_2$ is doomed, since what is semantically defective is not true.

Leaving this claim in abeyance for the moment, I now turn to an approach to resolving these paradoxes, derived from Tarski, for which the Strengthened Liar poses no special problem, no problem not already posed by the ordinary Liar. This approach also finds something semantically defective in sentences like L$_1$ ("L$_1$ is false") and L$_2$ ("L$_2$ is not true"), but of a quite different kind.

6   The reasoning depends on the equivalence between
       neither *P* nor *Q*
   and
       both not-*P* and not-*Q*.
   On what other principle does the reasoning depend?

5.5   Levels

In deriving apparently unacceptable conclusions from L_1 and L_2, we relied upon two principles:

> if a sentence is true, then things are as it says they are;
> if things are as a sentence says they are, then the sentence is true.

Tarski stressed the feature of truth these principles capture. He expressed it somewhat more formally. Let us use σ to stand in for a name of any sentence, and p to stand in for a sentence. Then, Tarski claimed, for any acceptable language we must accept every instance of

T σ is true iff p

provided that the sentence named by σ means the same as the sentence that replaces p. In the limiting case, these can be the same sentence; so an instance of T (putting "'Snow is white'" for σ and "snow is white" for p) is

"Snow is white" is true iff snow is white.

T may seem utterly platitudinous; but the Strengthened Liar shows that it has contradictory instances. Putting "L_2" for σ and "L_2 is not true" for p, we get:

(*) L_2 is true iff L_2 is not true.

Since L_2 is "L_2 is not true", (*) presumably meets the requirement that the sentence named by "L_2" (namely "L_2 is not true") means the same as the sentence which replaces p (namely "L_2 is not true").

One aspect of the problem posed by the Liar is that the apparently platitudinous T leads by apparently correct reasoning to the contradictory (*). Tarski's response is that the ordinary concept of truth, the one we use every day, is incoherent and must be rejected. According to Tarski, it needs to be replaced by a series of concepts of truth, hierarchically arranged, and each expressed in a language different from any natural language (i.e., from any language that has evolved naturally).

Suppose some language λ_0 contains a predicate "Tr_1" that applies to all and only the true sentences of λ_0. Suppose also that λ_0 contains a sentence σ that says of itself that it is not Tr_1. Then, granting T, we have a version of the Liar: if Tr_1 applies to σ, then σ says truly that Tr_1 does not apply to it; but if Tr_1 does not apply to it, then, since this is what it says, it is true, and so Tr_1 does apply to it. Tarski took the contradiction to refute the supposition that σ belongs to λ_0. The natural explanation of how this could be is that Tr_1 is not an expression of λ_0. Hence, no sentence belongs to λ_0 if it contains Tr_1. This blocks the paradox in the following sense: the proposed language, since it does not contain a predicate true just of its true sentences, is one in which the paradoxical sentence cannot be formulated. One can write down the words, but they are claimed to have no significance: they are semantically wholly defective.

We can enlarge a language by adding new expressions. In particular, we could enlarge λ_0, taken to contain no occurrence of "Tr_1", by adding "Tr_1". We could call the newly formed language λ_1: it contains all the sentences of λ_0, together with all sentences which can be formed from these by using "Tr_1"; so it contains σ. Paradox is still avoided: σ does not belong to λ_0, and since Tr_1 is defined only for λ_0 sentences, there is no question of Tr_1 applying to σ. The expression σ (= "σ is not Tr_1") does not belong to λ_0, and so it is not one of which "Tr_1" can be significantly affirmed or denied.

It is not that there is no predicate true of just the sentences of λ_1. There is: call it "Tr_2".[7] However, for familiar reasons, it cannot belong to λ_1.[8] In general, a predicate Tr_n cannot belong to a language λ_{n-1} but only to a language of level at least *n*.

No paradoxical Liar sentence can be formulated in any of the languages in Tarski's hierarchy. How is this supposed to provide a "solution" to the paradox? The paradox arises in our language, so a proper defusing of it must say something about our language, and not merely offer a replacement.

What Tarski says about our language is that the Liar shows it to be incoherent. We must replace our actual, but incoherent, concept of truth by a family of new concepts, each fixed to a level in the hierarchy, in the way just described. Many people have sought something less radical, a response that preserves more of our ordinary thought and talk.

One such less radical response draws on a Tarskian notion of hierarchy, but claims that this is already implicit in our actual use of "true". Unlike Tarski's account, which claimed that ordinary language is irremediably defective, this alternative claims that the defects are mere appearance: the underlying reality is that we already use a Tarski-like hierarchy of concepts of truth.

---

7 Is σ Tr_2?

8 How does the supposition that Tr_2 belongs to λ_1 lead to paradox?

A major difficulty with this suggestion is that there would appear to be nothing in our usage reflecting the appropriate sensitivity to Tarski-style, fixed-in-advance levels. For example, suppose I say:

What you said just now is not true.

On the face of it, anyone, including myself, could quite well know what I have said without knowing what you have said. (Imagine a game on the lines of paper, stone, and scissors: I have to guess whether what you have just written down is true or false.) On a hierarchical view in which levels are fixed in advance, something in my use of this sentence determines an association between "true" and some level. Presumably the normal (default) level would be 1. If you have said "Snow is white", there is no problem. But suppose you have said "What M. S. will say is true". On the present theory, the intelligibility of my utterance requires my "true" to be on a higher level than yours; but if my utterance can be understood without knowing what you have said, its level of truth must get fixed independently of the content of what you have said. This suggests that the attempt to apply this kind of hierarchy response to natural language is implausible. (However, compare Burge 1979.)

So far we have considered two main ways of making good the claim that Liar-paradoxical sentences are semantically defective. One used the notion of grounding, in terms of which there seemed to be some hope of defending the view that L_1 is neither true nor false; though the hope that this would lead to a resolution of all versions of the Liar was apparently dashed by the Strengthened Liar (L_2: L_2 is not true). The other was Tarski's claim that any non-hierarchical notion of truth is incoherent. The Strengthened Liar creates no special problem for this view.[9] However, it has

---

9   Why not? You might like to answer by criticizing one or both versions of the following reasoning:
Version 1:
Even when levels of truth are made explicit, as Tarski requires, we can formulate a Liar sentence, e.g.:
    L_N: L_N is not true$_n$.
If this is defective, through infringing levels requirements, then it is not true$_n$; but since this is what it says it is, it must be true$_n$ after all.
Version 2:
A sentence which violates levels is semantically defective and so not true; so one can always construct a Strengthened Liar sentence to refute a levels approach to the paradoxes. (Cf. the argument mentioned at the end of section 5.4 above.)

difficulties. To jettison our ordinary concept of truth seems too radical; yet it seems incorrect to suppose that our concept already contains, implicitly, the required segregation into levels. Where else might one look for an account of the semantic defectiveness of Liar sentences?

5.6   Self-reference

It is natural to think that something about the self-referential character of Liar paradoxical sentences is the main source of their paradoxical nature. There may be something in this thought, but as it stands it is both incorrect and inadequate.

It is incorrect because a sentence can refer to itself, as for example this very sentence does, without leading to any kind of semantic defect or paradox. So sentential self-reference cannot be the main source of Liar paradoxes.

It is inadequate because one can construct Liar paradoxes without using any sentence which refers to itself. One example of this phenomenon involves Liar cycles like the following.

(A)   (said by α on Monday): Everything β will say on Tuesday is true.

(B)   (said by β on Tuesday): Nothing α said on Monday is true. (Cf. Burge 1978, p. 90; he attributes the example to Buridan.)

If α and β said nothing other than, respectively, (A) and (B) on, respectively, Monday and Tuesday, we have a paradox of essentially the Liar type. Suppose (B) is true; then (A) is not true, and β will say something not true on Tuesday. Since β only says (B), (B) is not true. So if (B) is true, then it is not true. Suppose (B) is not true; then α said something true on Monday. Since α only said (A), (A) is true, that is, everything β will say on Tuesday is true. This includes (B), so (B) is true. Thus if (B) is not true, it is true.

Neither of the sentences in the story literally refers to itself. Rather, there is a kind of circle, so perhaps we should talk of "circular reference" rather than self-reference. However, as the circularity doesn't strictly involve reference at all, but rather quantification, it might be safer still just to speak of circularity.

We could expand the story of (A) and (B) by imagining a third utterance:

(C)   (said by γ on Tuesday): Nothing α said on Monday is true.

The fact that β and γ use the very same sentence, yet only one of them is circular in the relevant way, shows that circularity is not a property of sentences as such. Being meaningful or meaningless is a property of sentences. Since there is nothing paradoxical about (C), there is no reason to say it is other than meaningful, and since (B) is the same sentence, it follows that the property which circularity prevents is not that of being meaningful. We need a more refined notion, one sensitive to the use to which a sentence is put on a specific occasion. Such a notion emerges naturally from a consideration of indexicality; and the remaining two responses to the Liar which I shall consider both claim to discover, in reasoning related to the Strengthened Liar, some element of indexicality. One response locates the indexicality in the specific kind of self-reference involved in the Liar; the other, briefly mentioned in the last paragraph of section 5.8, locates it in the predicate "true".

To summarize: if we are to finger self-reference as the villain of the piece, the relevant kind of self-reference must contain an indexical element. However, once indexicality is allowed, we also open the way to a Tarski-like hierarchy of levels, triggered by indexical features of "true".

5.7   Indexicality

For reasons independent of Liar paradoxes, it is necessary to distinguish between sentences, regarded as things which can be uttered by different people and on different occasions, and the things which people can say or express by using sentences. The reason is the "indexicality" of language: the fact that the same words may, without exploiting ambiguity, be used on different occasions to say different things. Indexicality in pronouns provides a familiar example: if you use the sentence "I am hungry" affirmatively, you say one thing, and if I use it affirmatively I say another. The things said are different because it could be that what you say is true whereas what I say is false.

I will call what a sentence is used on a specific occasion to say or express a *statement*. Indexicality shows that it is only statements and not sentences that can properly be said to be true or false. I shall assume that bivalence holds for statements, so that every statement is either true or false. We have already in effect seen that a sentence can be meaningful, yet on a specific occasion be used in such a way as to fail to make a statement ("That elephant is about to charge"). Although sentences can be self-referential, or more generally can have the kind of circularity associated with paradox, it may be that statements cannot. Thus, reverting to the example in section 5.6 above, we might be able to justify the claim that whereas both β and γ use the same sentence, only γ thereby succeeds in making a statement. The notion of a statement thus seems to have the features we were looking for: it is a function not only of the meaning of a sentence, but also of the use to which it is put on a specific occasion.

The Strengthened Liar needs to be adapted to the distinction between sentence and statement. One way to do so is as follows:

L_2^* L_2^* does not express a true statement.

Reconsideration of the reasoning involved in the Strengthened Liar supports the view that some kind of indexicality is at work. We contemplate L_2^* and regard it as defective. When we come to express this, we may do so by words which are, or entail, L_2^* itself, for example: "L_2^* is semantically defective, so (*a fortiori*) it does not express a true statement; only the use of a non-defective sentence could do that." Intuitively this at first glance seems perfectly sensible (until we realize that we have ourselves re-used the very words we wish to say are defective). This intuition could be vindicated if we could show that the same words, even referring to the same thing, and applying the same predicate to it, may not say the same thing on two occasions of use. We want to say that the first use of L_2^* is defective, but the second use of those very words is not, since they are then used to express a truth.

The general feasibility of such an approach is suggested by considerations like the following. Suppose that the following sentence is the only sentence written on the board in room 101:

The sentence written on the board in room 101 does not express a true statement.

It appears perfectly consistent for me to write on this page that, because of some semantic defect, the sentence written on the board in room 101 does not express a true statement. I use the words which, as written on the board in room 101, are defective, in circumstances in which there is nothing defective about their use. This suggests that the same words, used to refer to the same thing, and applying the same predicate to it, do not necessarily make the same statement. The sentence written on the board in room 101 makes no statement, in its use in room 101; whereas I use those words, on this page, to make a true statement. I did not have to use the same words. Under suitable circumstances I could simply have said "*That* sentence does not express a true statement". That there are special circumstances under which I can re-use the same words is an accident of our use of language, and does not affect the truth of the statement I wish to make.

We are still some way from our goal, for three tasks remain: (i) to provide a more detailed account of what the problematic circularity is; (ii) to give some independent justification for saying that a statement cannot possess it; and (iii) to return to the problems posed by the Strengthened Liar.

5.8   Indexical circularity

For a specification and justification of the relevant kind of circularity, it is worth reverting to an idea of Bertrand Russell's, his so-called Vicious Circle Principle. He gives more than one account of what the principle is, but a fair statement (not a quotation) would be as follows:

> **VCP**   No totality can contain members fully specifiable only in terms of itself.

This is intended as a general metaphysical principle, applicable to classes as well as everything else, and thus also applicable to statements (or as Russell sometimes said, propositions).

The VCP gets no grip on totalities of straightforward material things, for none of these contain members which could be specified only in terms of themselves. We might specify Fred as the tallest man in the regiment, thus specifying him in terms of a totality to which he belongs, but it could not be that this is the *only* way in which he could be specified. The VCP has no tendency to wipe out regiments.

The VCP appears to get no grip on sentences, thought of as marks or shapes, for these, like members of regiments, can be specified in all sorts of independent ways, not all of which involve any kind of totality. In the case of statements, however, it does seem that some can only be fully specified in terms of a totality. Thus my statement that *everything you said in your radio talk was rubbish* can only be fully specified in terms of the totality of your statements. It can be incompletely or indirectly specified in other ways, for example, as the statement which resulted in the end of our friendship, or as the statement whose verbal expression occurs in italics on page 124 of *Paradoxes*. Full specification, however, does seem to involve collective mention of the things you said. In this case, there is no infringement of the VCP, since the totality of your statements does not include mine, and the totality of your statements together with mine is not the totality in terms of which my statement is specified (but is, rather, a larger one).

Is there a totality of statements specified by

$L_1^\dagger$ (The statement) $L_1^\dagger$ is false?

If so, it presumably contains the statement $L_1^\dagger$ as its only member. But $L_1^\dagger$ can only be fully specified in terms of that member. So the VCP rules that there is no such totality. Hence there is no such thing as the statement $L_1^\dagger$.

There seems to be some hope that the VCP could be extended to deal with Liar cycles, and thus that we could use it to accomplish our first task, that of specifying the nature of the problematic circularity. The second task is to give an independent motivation for saying that statements cannot possess the relevant kind of circularity. On this point, Russell offers us little by way of argument. The VCP is meant to seem independently acceptable, and is supposed to deliver appropriate restrictions. It is, I think, quite hard to find intuitively plausible considerations tending to show directly that statements cannot be circular in the problematic ways. (However, see Hossack, forthcoming.) One specific reason for concern is that a kind of circularity which would be precluded by the VCP has shown itself amenable to systematic mathematical treatment, namely, the kind of circularity involved in non-foundational set theory. (See Bibliographical Notes for a brief description and references.) So developing the idea that the root of the paradoxes lies with statement self-reference, or more generally statement circularity, requires work on this point.

Supposing that this can be successfully accomplished, will not the Strengthened Liar lie in wait to make the efforts pointless? The problem appears most threatening if we reconsider the sentence L_2^*:

L_2^* L_2^* does not express a true statement.

"L_2^*" labels a sentence, and the approach to the paradoxes under discussion wants to claim that it is a sentence which does not express a statement: thanks to circularity, it is semantically defective. Nothing which is semantically defective expresses a true statement, so in particular L_2^* *does not express a true statement*. The italicized words are just L_2^* itself, and we seem to have the makings of the familiar paradox.

The theorist must hold that his use of the words (as italicized) does express a statement, and a true one, and thus differs from the original use of these words. He could have made his point by using the non-paradoxical words "The sentence displayed above does not express a true statement". It is an accident of our labelling conventions that the very words to be condemned can be used to condemn them. In its defective use, L_2^* calls for the impossible, the existence of a self-referential statement; in its non-defective use it does not.

A solution of this kind ought to give rise to at least two kinds of worry. One is specific: could the ingenious opponent not devise Liar sentences for which this response is ruled out?[10] The other is more general: is the view consistent with the possibility of genuinely *formal* logic, logic in which the logical relations are mirrored by merely syntactic ones? If there is any looseness of fit, unamenable to theory, between sentences and statements, this project will be doomed.

The notion of indexicality can be exploited in a different way. We have explored the possibility that indexicality might affect the subject term in sentences like L_2 and L_2^*: whether or not the subject refers in a way demanding the existence of a self-referential statement was held to be a function of the circumstances of its use. One should also consider the possibility that indexicality affects the predicate term: "true". Tyler Burge (1979) has developed a suggestion on these lines. There are different levels of truth, and which level is at issue is fixed not by the meaning of the sentence, but by the statement it is used to make on a given occasion. This approach based on indexical levels avoids many of the difficulties associated with Tarski's hierarchy, which attaches to sentences rather than to statements. Burge's construction is complex, and I give no details here because I have the following suspicion: that it is hard or impossible to justify the claim that "true" is indexical, independently of the apparent need for it to be indexical to do justice to the paradoxes, whereas we have independent reason to believe in indexicality relating to self-reference.

5.9   Comparison: how similar are Russell's paradox and the Liar?

Are the two paradoxes of this chapter totally different, or essentially the same? Is the truth perhaps somewhere between these extremes?

Ramsey urged that the paradoxes are different in kind, and his view has been predominant, at least until relatively recently. He based the distinction on their different subject matter: the logical

---

[10]* Show how the response appears to be inadequate to:

No use of this very sentence expresses a true statement.

paradoxes, under which heading he included Russell's paradox, arise from logical notions, like that of class; the semantic paradoxes, under which he included the Liar, arise from semantic notions, like that of truth.

There are also structural dissimilarities, which might be traced to the difference in the concepts involved in the different paradoxes. There is no analogue in Russell's paradox of the Strengthened Liar. There is an immediate problem with the idea that *there is no* statement expressed by L_2, namely that it seems to follow that L_2 is not true. No such twist is consequent on the assertion that *there is no* class R. For the class paradox, there is quite widespread agreement on what we need to say – that there is no class R. What is unclear is how this can be justified. For the Liar, it is not clear even what ought to be said, let alone how to justify it.

However, the two paradoxes are also similar in many ways. I enumerate five.

(1) The Class paradox resembles a paradox about properties, and the Property paradox in turn resembles the Liar. Most properties are not true of themselves. For example, the property of being a man is not true of itself, since that property lacks the property of being a man; but the property of being a non-man is true of itself, since the property of being a non-man has the property of being a non-man. The pattern of reasoning used in the Class paradox would lead to the conclusion:

> The property of *being not true of itself* is true of itself if and only if it is not true of itself.

There is at least a surface similarity between this contradiction and the contradiction that L_2 truly predicates truth of itself if and only if it does not. Where the Property contradiction uses the notion of *not true of*, a relation that may hold between a property and something else (perhaps also a property), the Liar contradiction uses the notion of *not true*, a property that a sentence or statement may possess.

(2) Both the Class paradox and the Liar involve self-reference, or something like it.

(3) The principles appealed to in the derivation of the two paradoxes (CE: For every intelligible condition F, there is a class x, such that: for any object y, $y \, \varepsilon x$ if and only if y satisfies F; and T: σ is true iff p) are structurally similar, and appear to play similarly constitutive roles with respect to the intuitive notions of *class* and *truth*.

On the side of derivation, the comparison is this. The schema for any object y, $y \varepsilon x$ iff y is F

yields a contradiction when x is replaced by a name, say R, for the Russell class, and F by the condition, expressed in terms of this name, that supposedly defines membership for that class, "$\neg \varepsilon R$". Similarly, the schema

σ is true iff p

yields a contradiction when σ is replaced by a name, say L_2, for the Liar sentence, and p by the condition, expressed in terms of this name, that supposedly defines truth for that sentence, "L_2 is not true".

On the side of roles, the comparison is that just as CE appears constitutive of our pretheoretical notion of a class, so T appears constitutive of our pretheoretical notion of truth. CE determines what it is for a class to exist; T determines what it is for a truth condition to exist.

(4) Hierarchies have been used in response to both kinds of paradox, beginning with one of the earliest systematic treatments, in Russell (1908). It is natural to suppose that we should think of classes as constructed out of non-classes, with each constructional step drawing only upon entities which have already been constructed. Likewise, it is natural to suppose that we should think of statements ascribing truth as constructed out of statements free of the notion of truth, with each constructional step drawing only upon statements which have already been constructed.

(5) Russell's classification of the Class paradox and the Liar as of a common kind is based on the claim that they both alike derive from an infringement of the Vicious Circle Principle:

VCP   No totality can contain members fully specifiable only in terms of itself.

We have already seen how this might be invoked to ban certain kinds of circularity in statements. The way in which it bans circularity in classes is more straightforward. The specification of the class R, of non-self-membered classes, went like this:

For any class x, $x \varepsilon R$ iff $\neg x \varepsilon x$.

The specification speaks of what Russell would call a totality: the totality of all classes, introduced by the phrase "any class". Russell takes it that this is the only possible specification of R, and intends that the VCP tell us that R cannot belong to the totality introduced by the phrase "any class", as that occurs in the definition of R. For suppose R did belong to that totality; then the totality would contain a member R specifiable only in terms of that totality, which is what the VCP says is impossible. However, if R does not belong to the totality introduced by "any class", then we cannot make the usual move to the contradiction. The usual move goes like this: if the definition holds of *any class,* then in particular it holds of $R,$ so we can infer

$R \, \varepsilon \, R$ iff $\neg \, R \, \varepsilon R.$

The VCP has it that the totality introduced by *any class* excludes $R,$ so this reasoning is fallacious. In effect, the upshot of the VCP is that we cannot specify R as we had originally intended – in such a way, that is, that the question could arise about whether it has or lacks its defining property.

A formal vindication of Russell's claim that the paradoxes belong to a significant common kind has been provided by Priest (1994).

The Class and Liar paradoxes, like most things, are similar in some respects, dissimilar in others. So what? Classification matters here because of the constraints it imposes on proper responses to the paradoxes. (Many other paradoxes need to find their place in a classification: see Priest 1994.) If two paradoxes are *essentially* similar, similar in what really matters, then it is proper to respond in essentially similar ways. For example, if the Class paradox calls for a hierarchy of levels, and the Liar is essentially similar, then it too calls for a hierarchy of levels. If an adequate conception of classes should allow non-well-founded classes, e.g. the class α whose only member is $\alpha,$ and the Liar is essentially similar, then our response to it should allow for analogous circularity. Russell's allegedly common solution to the two paradoxes, his Ramified Theory of Types, has a somewhat specious uniformity, since some of its more complex features are motivated by matters relating to the Liar rather than the Class paradox.

To infer that paradoxes require a uniform solution, we must show more than that there is *a* kind to which the paradoxes belong. We have also to show that this kind reveals their common essential nature. I doubt, however, whether this can be done quite independently of views about what response is appropriate to each.

Bibliographical notes

Section 5.1
Russell's earliest published exposition of the Class paradox is in his (1903). For a historical overview, see van Heijenoort (1967). Most introductory logic texts have an account. For a fairly non-technical account, with the paradoxes firmly in mind, see Copi (1971). For a good and accessible introduction to set theory see Thomason (1970, chapter 13).

Current usage distinguishes between sets and classes: all sets are classes, but not all classes are sets. Intuitively, a set is a well-behaved class. The distinction presupposes a certain approach to the solution of Russell's paradox, and so is not appropriate to the present discussion.

The *power class* of a class is the class consisting of every sub-class of the class. Consider, for example, the class consisting of just the three elements *a, b,* and *c,* which we can write $\{a,b,c\}$. A class α is a subclass of a class β if and only if every member of α is a member of β. The class $\{a,b,c\}$ has the following subclasses: (1) $\wedge$ (the null class) – since $\wedge$ has no members, every member of $\wedge$ is a member of $\{a,b,c\}$; (2) $\{a\}$; (3) $\{b\}$; (4) $\{c\}$; (5) $\{a,b\}$; (6) $\{a,c\}$; (7) $\{b,c\}$; and (8) $\{a,b,c\}$ – since each member of this class is a member of $\{a,b,c\}$.

There are thus eight subclasses of a class with three members. So the class of all subclasses of $\{a,b,c\}$ is more numerous (by five members) than $\{a,b,c\}$ itself. Cantor's theorem holds obviously for classes with finitely many members. The interest of the theorem consists in the fact that it applies to classes of every cardinality.

A one–one function between two classes, α and β, associates each member of α with exactly one member of β, and each member of β with exactly one member of α. Cantor takes it that two classes have the same number of members (the same cardinality) if and only if there is a one–one function between them.

A good introduction to both kinds of paradoxes discussed in this chapter is Priest (1987): chapter 2 (set theoretic paradoxes) and chapter 1 (semantic paradoxes).

Section 5.2
Good starting points for the Liar: Mackie (1973); Prior (1961); Martin (1984, editor's introduction); Barwise and Etchemendy (1987, chapter 1).
For discussions of bivalence see Haack (1978) and Burge (1984).

Section 5.3
I borrow the word "grounding" and its cognates from Kripke (1975). I do not claim to have captured what he means by it, for his concept of grounding is embedded in a mathematical theory to which I cannot begin to do justice. However, the early part of his paper is perfectly accessible to the non-mathematician. A classic reference for grounding is Herzberger (1970).

Section 5.4
The expression "Strengthened Liar" originates with van Fraassen (1968), though the problem itself is much older.

Section 5.5
Tarski (1969) contains a semi-popular exposition of his views. The classic text is Tarski (1937); despite the technical nature of the main body of this piece, the first section is non-technical, accessible, and well worth reading. He sets out a condition of adequacy for a formal definition of truth (symbolized "Tr"), called Convention T, as follows:

> A formally correct definition of the symbol "Tr" ... will be called an ... *adequate definition of truth* if it has the following consequences:
> (α) all sentences which are obtained from the expression "x ε Tr if and only if p" by substituting for the symbol "x" a structural-descriptive name of any sentence of the language in question and for the symbol "p" the expression which forms the translation of this sentence into the metalanguage;
> (β) ... (pp. 187–8)

As it is sometimes put, Tarski allows us to draw on our intuitive conception of meaning (translation) in specifying the conditions for a correct definition of truth.

For a careful statement of Tarski's precise premises, together with a challenge to the full generality of the conclusion Tarski drew, see Gupta (1982, section II).

For each truth predicate in the hierarchy, Tarski accepts every instance of T. The fact that T has an inconsistent instance, if instances can be formed from any grammatically acceptable construction of English – in particular L_2 – is taken to show that there is no such coherent language as English. Replacing the single English predicate "true" by a hierarchy of truth predicates also involved, in Tarski's eyes, doing away with English, as normally understood.

Section 5.6
For an attack on self-reference, see Jørgensen (1953). For the claim that some kinds of self-reference are innocuous, see Barwise and Etchemendy (1987, esp. p. 15–6). For a collection on the topic, see Bartlett (1992).

Section 5.7
The classic source of the distinction between sentence and statement, advanced for reasons quite independent of the Liar, is Strawson (1950).

Section 5.8
The formulation of the VCP given on p. 124 is verbally closest to Russell (1908, p. 75). The justification for "only" comes from the formulation at p. 63 of that work; cf. Russell and Whitehead (1910–13, p. 37). I have used "fully specifiable" rather than Russell's "defined".

   Hazen (1987) traces the origin of responses of the general kind considered in this section to the fourteenth century philosopher, Jean Buridan. Hazen defends a version of the view considered here, and the approach has been taken by others, for example Goldstein (1992) and Hossack (forthcoming). For criticisms, see Hinkfuss (1991), Smiley (1993) (though he advances an account which centres on the idea that Liar sentences "malfunction"), and Priest (1993).

   To introduce non-foundational set theory, we think of a set in terms of a diagram. Thus the set consisting just of London and the set whose members are the number 7 and Mount Everest (conventionally written: {London, {7, Everest}}) can be represented by the diagram:

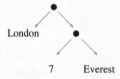

Here each blob represents a set, and the branches beneath it represent its members. The following diagram would then represent the set α whose only member is α:

The theory of such diagrams is consistent relative to classical set theory. A general account of the evils of circularity, like Russell's VCP, would do well to try to break the link between the diagrams and sets.

Non-foundational set theory owes a great deal to Aczel (1987). A good account, well adapted to present concerns, is in Barwise and Etchemendy (1987), chapter 3.

Section 5.9
Russell (1908) argues for the common nature of the Class, Liar and other paradoxes. For the distinction between logical and semantic paradoxes, see Ramsey (1925, pp. 171–2). The best exposition of the case for a single family of paradoxes is Priest (1994).

6.   Are any contradictions acceptable?

In previous chapters, I have at many points argued that if something seems to lead to a contradiction, then either it, or the relevant reasoning, must be rejected. The assumption that one must always reject contradictions has come under attack at various times in the history of philosophy. Very recently, the attack has taken a subtle form and has harnessed impressive technical resources.

I shall discuss the following views:

(1)   Some contradictions are true.
(2)   For some contradictions, it is rational to believe that they are true.

The only version of (1) that I shall consider also holds that every contradiction is false; this is "dialetheism". However, the view that some contradictions are both true and false does not add up to the view that some contradictions are acceptable, for one might go on to insist that anything perceived to be false should be rejected. If so, the assumption of the previous chapters of this book would remain unchallenged: we should reject anything which leads to a contradiction. So in this chapter I will discuss the conjunction of views (1) and (2). I shall call this combination "rational dialetheism".

The rational dialetheist's claim that some contradictions are true is, under natural assumptions, equivalent to the claim that some sentences are both true and false. Any such sentence may be called a *dialetheia*. I shall suggest in section 6.4 that, given natural assumptions, rational dialetheism entails that some sentences which are not contradictions (that is, are not of the form A and not-A) are both true and false.

The main positive case for dialetheism is that there is no better response to various paradoxes, notably, but not only, the Liar and Russell's paradox, than simply to accept the contradictions in question as true. So the main case for dialetheism is also a case for rational dialetheism. My discussion of the paradoxes of classes and of truth will no doubt have persuaded you that every solution faces difficulties; so you can imagine, in a general way, how one might make the case for simply accepting a contradiction. It is agreed by all parties that accepting a contradiction as true is a last resort. Dialetheists argue that we are forced to it; their opponents, that nothing could force us to it.

Once they have entered their positive case, in terms of the detailed discussion of various possible responses to paradoxes, dialetheists have to ward off objections. These can be divided into those that tell against both dialetheism and rational dialetheism, and those that tell only against the latter. Thus a case for rejecting all falsehoods could count against rational dialetheism without necessarily counting against dialetheism. However, a case against dialetheism is obviously a case against rational dialetheism. With some distress, I come to the conclusion that none of the objections I review ought to force a resourceful rational dialetheist to admit defeat.

6.1   Contradictions entail everything

Classical logic validates the inference rule (sometimes referred to by the scholastic term "ex contradictione quodlibet"): from a contradiction, anything may be derived. This is quite unproblematic for the classicist, since he holds that no contradictions are true. Although arguments with contradictory premises are classically valid, none of them are sound: we could never use them to derive anything, since we could never establish the premises.

As soon as one allows that there is even one true contradiction, the ex contradictione quodlibet rule would ensure that one would have a *sound* argument for any arbitrary proposition. One would be committed to holding that everything is true. This conclusion is absurd, and is accepted by dialetheists as absurd. They accordingly reject the classical inference rule.

Whatever one's final judgement upon dialetheism, one can but be impressed by how little need be lost by this modification of classical logic (Priest 1987).

Dialetheists need make no adjustment to the informal conception of validity: a valid argument is one which precludes the possibility of moving from truth to falsehood. In the classical picture, this conception validates the inference rule, since if a contradiction cannot be true, an argument whose premises include a contradiction is one whose premises cannot all be true, and thus is one which rules out the possibility of the argument leading from truth to falsehood.

Dialetheists, by contrast, do not assume that a contradiction cannot be true, and so are not committed to holding that every inference with a contradiction among its premises is valid.

6.2   A sentence which is both true and false could have no intelligible content

The meaning or content of a declarative sentence can be thought of in terms of which states of affairs would make it true, and which states of affairs would make it false. To understand a sentence, we must find out what it rules out, and what would rule it out. There are limiting cases: tautologies rule out nothing, and some sentences, ones which cannot be true, rule out everything. However, were there a sentence which is both true and false, there could be no coherent understanding of it, for there would be no determinate fact concerning what it ruled out, and what ruled it out. One would have to say: there is a state of affairs which the sentence both rules in and rules out. But this is like saying that the state of affairs both is and is not determined by the content of the sentence, which shows that the sentence has no coherent content at all.

These considerations are certainly not decisive. One way to bring this out is to rework them in terms of possible worlds semantics, as follows.

The content of a declarative sentence is given by two disjoint sets: the set of worlds at which it is true, and the set of worlds at which it is false. (This is one way of expressing one version of the view that the meaning of a sentence consists in the conditions under which it is true.) Suppose, for some sentence, the actual world belongs to the set of worlds at which it is true. Then it is not the case that the actual world belongs to the set of worlds at which it is false, since the set of worlds at which it is false is, by hypothesis, disjoint from the set of those at which it is true.

It is very plain that this kind of possible worlds semantics builds in the assumption that no sentence can be true or false, and provides not a shadow of an argument for it. It is not the mere fact of using possible worlds in the semantics which delivers the result. Rather, it is the assumption of disjointness of the set of worlds at which a sentence is true and the set of those at which it is false. There is nothing in the apparatus to prevent a sentence being associated by the semantics with a set of worlds at which it is true which overlaps the set of worlds at which it is false. To argue that no such association should be made requires philosophical work, which is not done merely by alluding to the apparatus.

If we now revert to the earlier formulation, in terms of what a sentence rules out, and what rules it out, the assumption which is hostile to dialetheism is that no meaningful sentence can rule something in which rules it out. This requires justification. It is not as if we cannot use the notions of ruling in and ruling out, just because of this overlap. The fault in the earlier argument is the assumption that if a sentence is both true and false, so that it rules in a state of affairs which rules it out, there is no "determinate" fact about what it rules in and what rules it out. The fact is determinate enough, but a fact at odds with anti-dialetheist presuppositions: that, determinately, some state of affairs is not ruled out by the sentence and that, determinately, the very same state of affairs rules the sentence out.

6.3   Three dualities

Assertion is an act, typically linguistic. When sincere, it expresses a mental state of acceptance on the part of the asserter towards what he asserts. Denial is likewise an act. When sincere, it expresses a mental state of rejection on the part of the asserter towards what he denies. We have three dualities which, in the best circumstances, seem as if they ought to line up: true/false; assert/deny; accept/reject. The alignment would be as follows: what is true is what is to be asserted and is what is to be accepted; what is false is what is to be denied and what is to be rejected.

According to Priest, if one does not accept A, there are two possibilities: rejecting A, which he characterizes as *refusing* to accept A, or being agnostic about A, neither accepting it nor refusing to accept it. Rejection and acceptance are thus not exhaustive; but he claims that they are exclusive: one cannot do both with respect to a single proposition at a single time. Yet, on his view, truth and falsehood are not exclusive: a single proposition may be both true and false at the same time. Are these views cotenable?

They confront a problem, if the following (or a close relative thereof) is true:

F   Anything false should be rejected.

For then all contradictions should be rejected (since they are all false), rejecting them makes it impossible to accept them (since rejection excludes acceptance), and it is hard to see how it could be rational to accept what it is impossible to accept.

F needs modification. It is not rational to reject what is in fact false, if all the available evidence suggests that it is true. However, the required modifications do not bear on the present discussion, so I shall ignore the need for them.

The argument may not be decisive, since perhaps we frail creatures are simply unable to do what an ideally rational agent would do, so what is "hard to see" may none the less be the case. However, there is some pressure upon the rational dialetheist to abandon F. This is the route taken by Priest, who points out that, for the rational dialetheist, rejecting all falsehoods would be incompatible with another ideal, that of accepting all truths. As he puts it:

> Truth and falsity come inextricably intermingled. ... One cannot, therefore, accept all truths and reject all falsehoods ... . (Priest 1986, p. 106; cf. Priest 1987, p. 124)

What one should do is to reject all falsehoods which are not also truths. This is a rule of conduct with which anti-dialetheists cannot quarrel, since from their perspective it is tantamount to F.

Priest allows that most of us, at one time or another, believe contradictions, that is, for some A, believe that A and also believe that not-A. It might seem that this will lead to trouble. If, for some A, we accept A and also accept not-A, we could sincerely assert not-A. So we could sincerely deny A. So we reject A. So there is a proposition we both accept and reject.

Priest disputes this reasoning, for he does not allow that one can infer that A is to be rejected from the premise that not-A is to be accepted. We will examine this issue more closely in the next section. Here I make two observations.

The first is that the exclusive character of acceptance and rejection is the impossibility of a person being in a state of acceptance and state of rejection with respect to a given proposition at a given time. This exclusiveness is not obviously inconsistent with it being demanded by rationality that one both accept and reject a given proposition at a given time. Ought does not imply can. Priest at one juncture appears favourably inclined to this strategy (1993, pp. 40–1). Its wholehearted endorsement would lead to some modifications to his earlier approach, as he himself notes.

The second observation is that Priest does not supply an argument for the exclusive character of acceptance and rejection, and one might be inclined to suppose that there exists an overlooked version of dialetheism, in which the attitudes are held to be compatible, and F is allowed.

The prospects for this version, however, are not bright, if the aim of providing a reasonable response to some of the paradoxes is to be retained. The idea is that when we come to a dialetheia, a proposition both true and false, we can accept it, and thus do not have to criticize the reasoning which led to it. If we were asked in addition to reject the dialetheia, then presumably it would be incumbent upon us to criticize the reasoning: reasoning from premises which must be accepted to a conclusion which must be rejected cannot be good. So adopting this strategy would leave dialetheists with at best a partial response to the paradoxes; they would have to go on, like everyone else, to say what is wrong with the reasoning.

This point also has an impact upon the version of dialetheism considered in the first observation. If we allow that we ought, rationally, to reject dialetheias as well as accept them, then we ought, rationally, to criticize the reasoning which led to them, and we would no longer have a satisfactory response to the paradoxes. In what follows, I shall accordingly treat dialetheists as holding to the exclusiveness of acceptance and rejection in a double sense: it is impossible for a person to be in both states with respect to one proposition at one time; and it is impossible that someone should be rationally required to be in both states with respect to one proposition at one time.

6.4   Negation

The dialetheist needs to say something about how negation relates to truth and falsehood, how it relates to acceptance and rejection, and how it relates to a proper account of our understanding of signs which express negation.

The first issue can be raised by considering an objection:

> Contradictions are conjunctions, having the form "A and not-A". A conjunction is true iff both conjuncts are. But "not-A" is true iff "A" is false. Hence we cannot have both "A" and "not-A" true; so no contradiction can be true.

The dialetheist can accept the premises of this argument (the one about conjunction, and the one about negation) and yet deny the conclusion. Suppose that "A" is false (as well as true). Then, by the rule for negation, "not-A" is true (as well as false). So, on the supposition, both conjuncts are true (as well as false). So, by the rule for conjunction, the conjunction is true (as well as false).

This shows that dialetheists must take it that some dialetheias are not explicitly of the form "A and not-A". (Examples are likely to include "Russell's class is a member of itself" and L_1 ("L_1 is false").) If there are any true contradictions, there must be some of the form "A and not-A" where "A" is restricted to non-contradictions. But if "*A*" has at most one truth value, "not-*A*" must have just the other truth value if it has any, so one must be other than true, so the contradiction could not be true. This reasoning depends upon the principles about conjunction and negation which formed the premises of the argument with which this section opened. We can conclude that the essence of dialetheism is that there are dialetheias; that there are true contradictions is, upon natural assumptions, a consequence.

As is plain from the response to the objection, Priest's view of the relation between negation and truth and falsehood coincides with that of the classical logician: not-*A* is true iff *A* is false; not-*A* is false iff *A* is true. However, the classical logician relates negation to acceptance and rejection by the following:

N   Something should be rejected iff its negation should be accepted.

Smiley (1993, p. 20) has claimed that N is in part constitutive of the concept of negation. Yet N cannot be accepted by dialetheists, given that they hold that rejection and acceptance are exclusive. If a contradiction should be accepted, so should both conjuncts, *A* and not-*A*. But if not-*A* should be accepted, it follows from N that *A* should be rejected, and so, given exclusiveness, that *A* should not be accepted.

Priest accepts part of N, viz.:

(N1)   If something should be rejected, its negation should be accepted.

However, he rejects the other part of N, viz.;

(N2)   Something should be rejected if its negation should be accepted.

The classical logician affirms N2 and the dialetheist denies it. As far as I can see, the position here is a stand-off, neither side being able to produce a non-question-begging argument for their view. Indeed, the position is, at least for a Priestian dialetheist, equivalent to the debate about F ("anything false should be rejected"). For if *A*'s negation is accepted, one is committed to accepting that *A* is false, so, by F, one should reject *A* (thus establishing N2 from F). If *A* is false, then it has a true negation, and so, according to Priest, a negation which should be accepted, and so, by N2, *A* itself should be rejected (thus establishing F from N2).

The questions of how negation relates to truth and falsehood, and to rejection and acceptance, are distinct from the final question about negation to be considered in this section: what is it for a person to understand some expression (e.g. "not" or "it is not the case that") as a sign for negation? The idea is to provide an account of what the person does in virtue of which he can be counted a party to the practice of using the expression in question as a sign of negation.

Here is one such account, which is hostile to dialetheism. To understand a sign for negation (e.g. "it is not the case that") is to know, for any sentence *A*, never to treat both "*A*" and "it is not the case that *A*" as true (Stephanou 1994). If this were a correct account, dialetheists would manifest a failure to understand negation. To put it another way, to suppose that there are dialetheias would be inconsistent with supposing that there is an intelligible sign for negation.

Doubtless, dialetheists will challenge the suggestion about what understanding a sign for negation consists in. However, making the minimal modification to the above account is probably not well advised. The minimal modification would identify understanding a sign of negation with knowing, for any sentence *A*, always to treat one of "*A*" and "it is not the case that *A*" as false. While this would eliminate the difficulty for dialetheism envisaged in the previous paragraph, another difficulty would arise. For what could treating a sentence as false amount to, other than rejecting it? On this account, it would seem that even if there were dialetheias, they would have to be rejected, so there would be no room for rational dialetheism.

The suggestion certainly does not count as a refutation of dialetheism. The very project of giving this kind of account of understanding an expression can be challenged. Even allowing the project, there is a good deal of room for manoeuvre in its execution. But we can at least discern a challenge for the dialetheist: to provide an account of what understanding negation involves.

6.5   Falsehood and untruth

For any predicate ϕ, we take it that we can form one which holds of just the things of which ϕ does not hold; or, at least, one which holds of just the things within the significance range of ϕ of which ϕ itself does not hold. Let us stipulate that "un" is an operator which has this effect. (We need not worry about whether this operator really surfaces in English, or whether it should count as a negation operator.) Then the set of happy things is disjoint from the set of unhappy things; the set of holy things disjoint from the set of unholy things; and the set of true things disjoint from the set of untrue things.

If we may stipulate thus, then we may form a Liar sentence for which dialetheism provides no adequate response:

L₃   This very sentence is untrue.

We cannot simply accept the reasoning which leads to the conclusion that the sentence is both true and untrue, for these, by hypothesis, are predicates with disjoint extensions. So even a dialetheist must criticize the reasoning. Dialetheism as such does not even address this paradox.

The objection is that even if we cannot disprove dialetheism by proving that "true" and "false" do not overlap, we can prove, because we can stipulate, that "true" and "untrue" do not overlap. This allows us to create a paradox, closely similar to familiar Liar paradoxes (perhaps identical to the Strengthened Liar), which the dialetheist cannot address. This does not show that dialetheism is incorrect. It is consistent with the view that some contradictions are true. But it does show, supposedly, that allowing that some contradictions are true will not do all the work that dialetheists had hoped it would. Moreover, given the similarities among the semantic paradoxes, it suggests that another approach will need to be found to all of them.

The dialetheist might simply accept this objection, stressing that it relates not to the truth of dialetheism, but only to the extent of its application. Alternatively, he might resist the charge. "L₃ is true and L₃ is untrue" is, to be sure, a contradiction; but it is one for which we have powerful arguments, so why should it not be one of the true contradictions? If "L₃ is true" is false, then "L₃ is untrue" can be true; so if, in addition, "L₃ is true" is true, we have what is required for a true contradiction.

This reply in effect commits the dialetheist to the claim that truth and untruth are non-exclusive, as well as exclusive. Priest agrees (1987, pp. 90–1). Arguing that L₃ shows that some sentences are true as well as untrue (thus establishing non-exclusiveness), he also argues that from the law of excluded middle, which he accepts, one can derive that everything is either true or untrue, which entails that nothing is both true and untrue (thus establishing exclusiveness). Thus he accepts that the machinery he brings to bear upon the nature of contradictions is itself contradictory.

Whether this is tolerable is too large an issue for me to address. However, I will close with one observation on behalf of the dialetheist. I opened this section by imagining a stipulation to the effect that "untrue" would be a predicate with an extension disjoint from "true". I hoped my readers would accept this proposal without a qualm, and thus take it that there could be no question of overlap between "true" and "untrue". My closing remark is simply that confidence of this kind is not in general justified. Wanting our stipulations to be consistent is not enough to ensure that they are, as will be obvious to anyone familiar with legal stipulations. Our use of "true" is governed by certain principles, and there is no *a priori* guarantee that these principles permit a non-contradictory stipulation of a disjoint predicate.

The discussion has been inconclusive: I have not been able to show that dialetheism is incorrect. If it is correct, then it should be considered a candidate in connection with most of the paradoxes discussed in this book.

An inconclusive discussion may, none the less, be worthwhile. As Priest says:

> ... whether or not dialetheism is correct, a discussion of the questions it raises, concerning fundamental notions like negation, truth and rationality ... can hardly fail to deepen our understanding of these notions. (Priest 1993, p. 35)

Bibliographical notes

For the early history of dialetheism, see the editors' introduction to Priest, Routley, and Norman (1989). The word was coined by Priest and Routley in the early nineteen eighties. The most important reference is Priest (1987). His defence of dialetheism involves some excellent discussions of many paradoxes relating to classes and truth, since motivating his own view requires showing that alternative responses to them are inadequate. See also his symposium with Smiley (1993), which I have used as the basis of much of this chapter; and Rescher and Brandom (1980).

The expression "rational dialetheism" was suggested to me by Priest (personal communication).

Its being rational to hold dialetheism does not entail rational dialetheism, any more than its being rational to believe that Tom loves someone entails, concerning some person, that it is rational to believe that Tom loves that person.

Horn (1989) suggests that there are different kinds of negation. This idea would need to be considered in a full account of the relation between negation and rejection.

Stephanou (1994) does not endorse the suggestion about understanding negation which I discuss.

Appendix I   Some more paradoxes

(An asterisk before a title indicates that there is an observation on the entry in Appendix II.)

The Gallows

The law of a certain land is that all who wish to enter the city are asked to state their business there. Those who reply truly are allowed to enter and depart in peace. Those who reply falsely are hanged. What should happen to the traveller who, when asked his business, replies, "I have come to be hanged"?

Buridan's Eighth Sophism

Socrates in Troy says, "What Plato is now saying in Athens is false". At the same time, Plato in Athens says, "What Socrates is now saying in Troy is true". (Cf. Buridan, in Hughes 1982, pp. 73–9.)

The Lawyer

Protagoras, teacher of lawyers, has this contract with pupils: "Pay me a fee if and only if you win your first case". One of his pupils, Euathlus, sues him for free tuition, arguing as follows: "If I win the case, then I win free tuition, as that is what I am suing for. If I lose, then my tuition is free anyway, since this is my first case."

Protagoras, in court, responds as follows: "If you give judgment *for* Euathlus, then he will owe me a fee, since it is his first case and that was our agreement; if you give judgment for me, then he will owe me a fee, since that is the content of the judgment."

The Designated Student

Five students are told by the teacher that all of them are to have a star pinned on their backs; that just one of the stars is gold – the recipient of this is the "designated student"; and that the designated student will not know he or she is designated. The students are lined up so that the fifth can see the backs of the other four, the fourth the backs of the other three, and so on.

They argue that what the teacher said cannot be true, for the following reasons:

> The fifth student can infer that he cannot be unknowingly designated, since, if he were designated, he could see, from the non-gold nature of the stars on the other students, that none of them is designated, and thus could infer that he himself is designated.
> The fourth student can infer that (a) the fifth student cannot be unknowingly designated and (b) the fourth cannot be either, since, given that the fifth has not been designated, the fourth would be able to infer, from the non-gold nature of the three visible backs, that he was designated, if he was.
> ... and so on.

Is this a genuine paradox? Is it a version of the Unexpected Examination? (See Sorensen 1982.)

*The Grid

The following paradox has been said to be structurally like the Unexpected Examination. Is it? Does it contain a serious paradox?

In the Grid game, you are blindfolded and placed on a grid with numbered squares as shown in the diagram:

1	2	3
4	5	6
7	8	9

The double outer line represents a wall. You are allowed to move only horizontally or vertically, and you may attempt only two moves from your initial position. Your aim is to determine which square you are on. You might be lucky. For example, if you attempt a move right and feel the wall, then attempt a move down and feel the wall, you can infer that you are placed on square 9. However, you might be unlucky. For example, if you moved left twice without reaching the wall, you could not tell whether your initial position was 6, 3, or 9.

Suppose I claim that I can put you in an initial position not discoverable in two moves. However, you reason as follows: I cannot be put in any of the corner squares, since there are two-move sequences (like the one mentioned for square 9) that would tell me where I am; but if 1, 3, 7, and 9 can be eliminated, so can 2, 4, 6, and 8, since, for example, a move up into the wall would tell me that I was at 2, given the elimination of 1 and 3 as possibilities. Hence my initial position must be 5, and so I *can* discover my initial position – and in zero moves! (See Sorensen 1982.)

*The Stone

Can an omnipotent being make a stone so heavy that he cannot lift it? He can, because, being omnipotent, he can do everything. However, he also cannot, since, if he could make it, there would be something he could *not* do – that is, lift it. Reading: Savage (1967); Schrader (1979); and, for a variant, Mele and Smith (1988).

Heterological

Let us call an expression "heterological" if and only if it does not describe itself. Thus "long" is heterological because

　　"long" is long

is false; but "short" is not heterological since

　　"short" is short

is true. Is "heterological" heterological or not?

We could shorten the definition to the following schema, abbreviating "heterological" as "het":

　　het("φ") iff $\neg\varphi$("φ").

The contradiction follows immediately by taking "het" as the replacement for the schematic φ. Reading: Russell (1908); Quine (1966, esp. pp. 4ff, "Grelling's Paradox").

*The Lottery

Suppose there are a thousand tickets in a lottery and only one prize. It is rational to believe of each ticket that it is very unlikely to win. Hence it must be rational to believe that it is very unlikely that any of the thousand tickets will win – that is, rational to believe that it is very unlikely that there will be a winning ticket.

The Preface

Knowing one's frailties as one does, it is rational to suppose that one's book contains errors, and it is not unknown for authors to say as much in their prefaces. However, a sincere author will believe everything asserted in the text. Rationality, plus modesty, thus forces such an author to a contradiction. (Cf. Makinson 1965.)

The Preface Again

Suppose an author's preface consists solely in this remark: "At least one statement in this book is false". Then the body of the book must contain at least one false statement. For suppose it does not. Then if the preface is true, it is false, and if it is false, it is true; which is impossible. (Cf. Prior 1961, pp. 85–6.)

The Infallible Seducer

An unsuccessful wooer was advised to ask his beloved the following two questions:

(1)   Will you answer this question in the same way that you will answer the next?
(2)   Will you sleep with me?

If she keeps her word, she must answer Yes to the second question whatever she has answered to the first.

This paradox is amusingly generalized in Storer (1961).

Buridan's Tenth Sophism

Suppose that:

A is thinking that $2 + 2 = 4$.
B is thinking that dogs are reptiles.
C is thinking that an odd number of the current thoughts of A, B, and C are true.

Is what C thinks true or not? See Buridan, in Hughes (1982, p. 85), Prior (1961), Burge (1978, p. 28).

Forrester's Paradox

Suppose Smith is going to murder Jones. It is obligatory that if he murders Jones, he should do so gently. This appears to imply that if Smith murders Jones, it is obligatory that he do so gently. However, he cannot murder Jones gently without murdering him. Hence, given that Smith is going to murder Jones, it is obligatory that he do so. (See Forrester 1984.)

The Chooser

Someone whom you trust implicitly presents you with a choice: you can take either or both of box *A* or box *B*. Whatever happens, there is $100 in box *B;* moreover, there will be in addition $10,000 in box *A* if and only if you choose irrationally. What should you do? Cf. Gaifman (1983).

Bertrand's Paradox

What is the probability that a random chord of a circle exceeds the side of an inscribed equilateral triangle? It is longer if its midpoint lies on the inner half of the radius bisecting it; so, since the midpoint may lie anywhere on this radius, the probability is one-half. It is also longer if its midpoint lies within a concentric circle with half the original radius; so, since the area of this inner circle is a quarter that of the original circle, the probability is one-quarter.

*This Is Nonsense

> Line 1:   The sentence written on Line 1 is nonsense.
> Line 2:   The sentence written on Line 1 is nonsense.

For a suitable interpretation of "nonsense," we incline to believe that the sentence on Line 2 is true: the sentence it refers to is viciously self-referential, deserves to fall in the truth-value gap, or whatever. Yet the sentence on Line 2 is the very sentence it so justly criticizes.

The example comes from Gaifman (1983).

*The Penny Game

A game for two players. Playing in turn, either player may take one or two pennies from a pile before them. Any penny taken belongs to the player who takes it. Any pennies left in the pile when the game is over vanish. The game stops either when there are no pennies left in the pile, or after a player takes two pennies in one turn.

The paradoxical conclusion is that if both players are rational, and know it (of themselves and of each other) the first player will take two pennies, thus ending the game. The conclusion is paradoxical because one would think that two rational people ought to end up splitting the pot, for then both would be better off. (And if rationality doesn't help you satisfy your desires, what's the point of it?)

An argument for the conclusion goes as follows. Suppose there are just two pennies left at your turn. If you take one penny, then the other player will take the last penny, and the game will end, with you gaining just one penny. This is less good than if you had taken two pennies. The game would end then, but you would have gained one penny rather than two.

Now suppose that there are three pennies left. If you take just one penny, you will leave the other player with two pennies. You know that the other player is rational, and so will do the rational thing, and you have just worked out that the rational thing, faced with two pennies, is to take two. So if, faced with three pennies, you take just one, you know that the game will end after the next move, and you will gain only one penny. By contrast, if you take two pennies now, you will gain two pennies rather than one.

The argument iterates backwards, regardless of how many pennies there are in the pile.

See Hollis and Sugden (1993).

Appendix II Remarks on some text questions and appended paradoxes

Remark numbers refer to footnote numbers in the given chapter.

Chapter 1. Zeno's paradoxes: space, time and motion

2. One possible argument is this. If there were as many as two things, say α and β, then we could consider the whole W formed by these two things. Then W has α and β as its parts. So if nothing has parts, there are not as many as two things, i.e., there is at most one thing.

6. Yes, it does mean that the button will travel faster than the speed of light. Whether or not this is a logical possibility could be disputed, but it is fairly uncontroversial that it is not impossible *a priori;* that is, reasoning alone, unaided by experiment, cannot establish that nothing can travel faster than light.

8. "Going out of existence at Z^*" might mean "Z^* was the last point occupied" or, alternatively, "Z^* was the first point not occupied". The latter serves Benacerraf's cause against the objection.

Chapter 2. Vagueness: the paradox of the heap

9. He should deny the first premise. Since he believes that there are no heaps, he will think that it is false that a 10,000-grained collection is a heap. This shows that one should treat with care the taxonomy of responses described in the text. Unger's position, though in a sense unified, must be regarded as accepting the conclusion of some soritical arguments and denying the premises of others.

Chapter 3. Acting rationally

3.   If a person's utilities can be measured in cash value terms, then his or her utilities are "commensurable": of any two possible circumstances, either one has more utility than the other, or else they are of equal utility. However, if we think of very disparate "utilities", it may be not merely that we do not *know* how they compare, but that there is no such thing as how they compare. For an early defence of commensurability see Rashdall (1907, chapter 2). For a recent discussion see Nussbaum (1986, esp. pp. 107ff.).

4.   It would seem that it could not as it stands, for the following reason. The outcome of a gamble, in cash terms, does not register the fact that it is obtained by gambling. A given sum has the utility it has, whether earned or won. So what would be needed, to register a dislike of gambling, would be a "higher order" conception of utility. The expected utilities delivered by the MEU as it stands would be subjected to a weighting, which would augment expected utilities whose probability component is high, and diminish those whose probability component is low.

5.   The example shows that the dominance principle does not issue in guidance about which actions are rational, unless it is combined with instructions about how the possible outcomes should be divided up.

17.   Each reasons as follows: "In the *last* game it will be best for me to confess, since any loss of trust this induces will be irrelevant, as we are not going to 'play' again." However, the other can work this out and will adopt the same strategy: "Since he will confess in the *last* game, I should confess in the penultimate game, since any loss of trust this may induce will be irrelevant" (and so on).

Chapter 4. Believing rationally

3.   It might be that the conditions for evidence being good could not be known to obtain.

5.   "All emeralds are green" and "All emeralds are grue" are not, strictly, inconsistent. If there were no unexamined emeralds, both generalizations would be true; whereas it is impossible for genuinely inconsistent propositions both to be true.
      A given body of evidence can "point both ways", i.e., can provide grounds for two propositions that are genuinely in-

consistent. In such cases, the evidence can normally be divided into evidence that supports the one proposition, and evidence that supports the other, without overlap (at least, without total overlap). What is paradoxical about the grue case is that no such division is possible: divide the evidence as fine as you like, every bit that confirms "All emeralds are green" also confirms "All emeralds are grue".

Chapter 5. Classes and truth

3. Suppose L_1 is not false, that is, suppose not-L_1. (Principle: since L_1="L_1 is false" we may substitute one for the other. For an attack on the use of this principle, see Skyrms (1982).) Then not-L_1 is, by supposition, true. So L_1 is false. (Principle: a sentence is false if its negation is true.) So if L_1 is not false, it is false. So it is false. But since this is what L_1 says it is, it is true. So it is both true and false.

5. Suppose L_1 is false; then it tells it the way it is, so it is true, and hence *L_1 is not false*. (Principle: Anything true is not false.) Cf. Martin (1984, pp. 2–3).

10. Call the sentence "No use of this very sentence expresses a true statement" S. Consider an arbitrary use U_1 of S. If U_1 succeeds in making a true statement, then it does not make a true statement (since it says that *no* use of S expresses a truth). So U_1 does not make a true statement. But if this were generally true, of all uses of S, U_1 would be true after all. So there must be a U_2 which does make a true statement. But this leads to a contradiction. Cf. Hazen (1987); for a criticism, see Hinkfuss (1991); see also Smiley (1993).

Appendix I

The Grid
The alleged paradox seems to turn on an equivocation between whether there is a sequence of moves that fixes one's position, and whether every possible sequence does so. There is no corresponding equivocation in the Unexpected Examination. (But see Sorensen 1982.)

The Stone
No, an omnipotent being cannot make a stone so heavy that he cannot lift it. He will still be omnipotent with respect to making and lifting stones, however, if for any weight of stone (in grammes,

megatons, or whatever) he can make one of that weight and lift one of that weight. However, see Mele and Smith (1988).

The Lottery

One suggestion is that this shows that one may have good reason for believing that *A* and good reason for believing that *B,* yet not have good reason for believing that *A* and *B.* This suggestion would need to be supplemented by a treatment of sorites-style reasoning based on: "If one has good reason to believe a proposition with probability *n,* then one has good reason to believe a proposition with probability minutely smaller than *n.*"

This Is Nonsense

The example supports the view that two sentence-tokens of a single sentence-type can differ in truth value (one true, the other not) even if both refer to the same thing and predicate the same property of it.

The Penny Game

This has the structure of a multiple Prisoner's Dilemma, which is known by the parties to have finitely many iterations. Compare chapter 3, note 17 (p. 71), and the comment above (p. 152).

Bibliography

Aczel, Peter (1987) *Lectures on Nonwellfounded Sets.* Stanford, Calif. CSLI Lecture Notes, No 9.

Anand, Paul (1993) *Foundations of Rational Choice Under Risk.* Clarendon Press, Oxford.

Aristotle, *Physics*, trans. W. Charlton. Oxford University Press, Oxford. 1970.

Asher, Nicholas M., and Kamp, Johan A. W. (1986) "The knower's paradox and representational theories of the attitudes." In J. Halpern, ed., *Theoretical Aspects of Reasoning about Knowledge.* Morgan Kaufman, New York, pp. 131–48.

Axelrod, R. (1984) *The Evolution of Cooperation.* Basic Books, New York.

Bar-Hillel, Maya, and Margalit, Avishai (1972) "Newcomb's paradox revisited." *British Journal for Philosophy of Science* 23: 295–304.

(1983) "Expecting the unexpected." *Philosophia* 13: 263–88.

(1985) "Gideon's paradox – a paradox of rationality." *Synthese* 63: 139–55.

Bartlett, Steven J. (1992) *Reflexivity: A Source-Book in Self-Reference.* North-Holland, Amsterdam and London.

Barwise, Jon, and Etchemendy, John (1987) *The Liar: An Essay in Truth and Circularity.* Oxford University Press, New York & Oxford.

Benacerraf, Paul (1962) "Tasks, super-tasks, and the modern Eleatics." *Journal of Philosophy* 59: 765–84. Reprinted in W. Salmon (1970), pp. 103–29.

Benditt, T.M., and Ross, David J. (1976) "Newcomb's paradox." *British Journal for the Philosophy of Science* 27: 161–4.

Black, Max (1937) "Vagueness: an exercise in logical analysis." *Philosophy of Science* 4: 427–55. Reprinted in his *Language and Philosophy.* Cornell University Press, Ithaca, N.Y. 1949, pp. 25–58.

(1967) "Probability." In Edwards (1967), pp. 464–79.

Burge, Tyler (1978) "Buridan and epistemic paradox." *Philosophical Studies* 34: 21–35.

(1979) "Semantical paradox." *The Journal of Philosophy* 76: 169–98. Reprinted in Martin (1984), pp. 83–117.

(1984) "Epistemic paradox." *The Journal of Philosophy* 81: 5–29.

Buridan, John *Sophismata*. See Hughes (1982).

Campbell, Richmond, and Sowden, Lanning, eds. (1985) *Paradoxes of Rationality and Cooperation: Prisoner's Dilemma and Newcomb's Problem*. University of British Columbia Press, Vancouver.

Cargile, J. (1965) "The sorites paradox." *British Journal for the Philosophy of Science* 20: 193–202.

Copi, Irving M. (1971) *The Theory of Logical Types*. Routledge and Kegan Paul, London.

Dummett, Michael (1975) "Wang's paradox." *Synthese* 30: 301–24. Reprinted in his *Truth and Other Enigmas*. Duckworth, London. 1978, pp. 248–68.

Edgington, Dorothy (1992) "Validity, uncertainty and vagueness." *Analysis* 52.4: 193–204.

Edwards, Paul (1967) *The Encyclopedia of Philosophy*. Collier–Macmillan and The Free Press, New York.

Evans, Gareth (1978) "Can there be vague objects?" *Analysis* 38: 208. Reprinted in his *Collected Papers*. Oxford University Press, Oxford. 1985, pp. 176–7.

Fine, Kit (1975) "Vagueness, truth and logic." *Synthese* 30: 265–300.

Fitch, F. (1952) *Symbolic Logic*. The Ronald Press Company, New York.

Forrester, James William (1984) "Gentle murder and the adverbial samaritan." *Journal of Philosophy* 81: 193–7.

Foster, John (1983) "Induction, explanation and natural necessity." *Proceedings of the Aristotelian Society* 83: 87–101.

Foster, Marguerite, and Martin, Michael L., eds. (1966) *Probability, Confirmation and Simplicity*. Odyssey Press, New York.

Gaifman, Haim (1983) "Paradoxes of infinity and self-application, I." *Erkenntnis* 20: 131–55.

Gale, Richard M., ed. (1968) *The Philosophy of Time*. Macmillan, London.

Gibbard, A., and Harper, W.L. (1978) "Counterfactuals and two kinds of expected utility." In C. A. Hooker, J. J. Leach, and E. F. McClennon, eds., *Foundations and Applications of Decision Theory,* vol. I. Reidel, Dordrecht, pp. 125–62. Reprinted (abridged) in Campbell and Sowden (1985), pp. 133–58.

Goguen, J.A. (1969) "The logic of inexact concepts." *Synthese* 19: 325–78.

Goldstein, Laurence (1992) "'This statement is not true' is not true." *Analysis* 52.1: 1–5.

Goodman, Nelson (1955) *Fact, Fiction and Forecast*. Harvard University Press, Cambridge, Mass.; 2nd ed., Bobbs-Merrill, Indianapolis, 1965.

(1978) *Ways of Worldmaking*. Hackett, Indianapolis.

Grünbaum, Adolf (1967) *Modern Science and Zeno's Paradoxes.* Wesleyan University Press, Middletown, Conn.

Gupta, Anil (1982) "Truth and paradox." *Journal of Philosophical Logic* 11: 1–60. Reprinted in Martin (1984), pp. 175–235.

Haack, Susan (1978) *The Philosophy of Logics.* Cambridge University Press, Cambridge.

Hazen, Allen (1987) "Contra Buridanum." *Canadian Journal of Philosophy* 17: 875–80.

Hempel, Carl (1945) *Aspects of Scientific Explanation and Other Essays in the Philosophy of Science.* The Free Press, New York. Reprint ed., 1965. The material on the Ravens Paradox is reprinted from *Mind* 54: 1–26, 97–121 (1945).

Herzberger, Hans A. (1970) "Paradoxes of grounding in semantics." *The Journal of Philosophy* 67: 145–67.

Hinkfuss, Ian (1991) "Pro Buridano; contra Hazenum." *Canadian Journal of Philosophy* 21.3: 389–98.

Hollis, Martin and Sugden, Robert (1993) "Rationality in action." *Mind* 103: 1–35.

Horn, L. R. (1989) *A Natural History of Negation.* University of Chicago Press, Chicago.

Hossack, Keith (forthcoming) "Materialism, dualism and the Liar paradox."

Hughes, G. E., ed. and trans. (1982) *John Buridan on Self-Reference.* Cambridge University Press, Cambridge & New York. This work by Buridan was originally entitled *Sophismata*.

Hume, David (1738) *A Treatise of Human Nature.*

Hyde, Dominic (1994) "Why higher-order vagueness is a pseudo-problem." *Mind* 103: 35–41.

Jackson, Frank (1975) "Grue." *Journal of Philosophy* 72: 113–31.

Janaway, Christopher (1989) "Knowing about surprises: a supposed antinomy revisited." *Mind* 98: 391–409.

Jeffrey, Richard C. (1965) *The Logic of Decision.* McGraw-Hill, New York.

Jørgensen, Jørgen (1953) "Some reflections on reflexivity." *Mind* 62: 289–300. Reprinted in Bartlett (1992), pp. 63–74.

Kamp, Hans (1975). "Two theories about adjectives." In E. Keenan, ed., *Formal Semantics of Natural Language.* Cambridge: Cambridge University Press, pp.123–55.

(1981) "The paradox of the heap." In U. Monnich, ed., *Aspects of Philosophical Logic.* Reidel, Dordrecht, pp. 225–77.

Koons, Robert (1992) *Paradoxes of Rationality.* Cambridge University Press, Cambridge.

Kripke, Saul (1975) "Outline of a theory of truth." *The Journal of Philosophy* 72: 690–716. Reprinted in Martin (1984), pp. 53–81.

(1982) *Wittgenstein on Rules and Private Language.* Blackwell, Oxford.

Kyburg, Henry (1961) *Probability and the Logic of Rational Belief.* Wesleyan University Press, Middletown, Conn.

Levi, Isaac (1967) *Gambling with Truth.* Routledge and Kegan Paul, London.

Lewis, David (1979) "Prisoner's Dilemma is a Newcomb problem." *Philosophy and Public Affairs* 8: 235–40. Reprinted in Campbell and Sowden (1985), pp. 251–5.

(1988) "Vague identity: Evans misunderstood." *Analysis* 48: 128–30.

Mackie, J.L. (1973) *Truth, Probability and Paradox.* Oxford University Press, Oxford.

(1977) "Newcomb's paradox and the direction of causation." *Canadian Philosophical Review* 7: 213–25. Reprinted in his *Collected Papers II.*

Makinson, D. C. (1965) "The paradox of the preface." *Analysis* 25: 205–7.

Martin, Robert L., ed. (1984) *Recent Essays on Truth and the Liar Paradox.* Oxford University Press, Oxford.

Mele, Alfred R. and Smith, M.P. (1988) "The new paradox of the stone." *Faith and Philosophy* 5: 283–90.

Mellor, D.H. (1971) *The Matter of Chance.* Cambridge University Press, Cambridge & New York.

Montague, Richard, and Kaplan, David (1960) "A paradox regained." *Notre Dame Journal of Formal Logic* 1: 79–90. Reprinted in Richmond Thomason, ed., *Formal Philosophy.* Yale University Press, New Haven. 1974, pp. 271–85.

Nozick, R. (1969) "Newcomb's problem and two principles of choice." In Nicholas Rescher, ed., *Essays in Honor of Carl G. Hempel.* Reidel, Dordrecht. Abridged version reprinted in Campbell and Sowden (1985), pp. 107–33.

(1993) *The Nature of Rationality.* Princeton University Press, Princeton.

Nussbaum, Martha C. (1986) *The Fragility of Goodness: Luck and Ethics in Greek Tragedy and Philosophy.* Cambridge University Press, Cambridge & New York.

Parfit, Derek (1984) *Reasons and Persons.* Oxford University Press, Oxford.

Peacocke, C. A. B. (1981) "Are vague predicates incoherent?" *Synthese* 46: 121–41.

Peirce, C. (1935) *The Collected Papers of Charles Sanders Peirce.* Charles Hartshorne and Paul Weiss, eds. Harvard University Press, Cambridge, Mass.

Priest, Graham (1986) "Contradiction, belief and rationality." *Proceedings of the Aristotelian Society* 86: 99–116.

(1987) *In Contradiction.* Nijhof, Dordrecht.

(1993) "Can contradictions be true?" *Supplementary Proceedings of the Aristotelian Society* 67: 35–54.

(1994) "The structure of the paradoxes of self-reference." *Mind* 103: 25–34.

Priest, Graham, Routley, Richard and Norman, Jean, eds. (1989) *Paraconsistent Logic: Essays on the Inconsistent.* Philosophia Verlag, Munich.

Prior, Arthur N. (1961) "On a family of paradoxes." *Notre Dame Journal of Formal Logic* 2: 16–32.

(1971) *Objects of Thought.* Oxford University Press, Oxford.

Quine, Willard van O. (1953) "On a so-called paradox." *Mind* 62: 65–7. Reprinted in his (1966), pp. 19–21.

(1966) *Ways of Paradox and Other Essays.* Random House, New York. (The title essay is on pp. 1–18.)

Ramsey, Frank P. (1925) "The foundations of mathematics." Reprinted in D. H. Mellor, ed. *Foundations.* Humanities Press, Atlantic Highlands, N.J. 1978, pp. 152–212.

(1926) "Truth and probability." Reprinted in D. H. Mellor, ed., *Foundations.* Humanities Press, Atlantic Highlands, N.J. 1978, pp. 58–100.

Rashdall, Hastings (1907) *The Theory of Good and Evil,* vol. II. Oxford University Press, London.

Rescher, N., and Brandom, R. (1980) *The Logic of Inconsistency.* Blackwell, Oxford.

Russell, Bertrand (1903) *The Principles of Mathematics.* Cambridge University Press, Cambridge & New York.

(1908) "Mathematical logic as based on the theory of types." *American Journal of Mathematics* 30: 222–62. Reprinted in R. C. Marsh, ed. *Logic and Knowledge.* Allen and Unwin, London. 1956, pp. 59–102.

(1936) "The Limits of Empiricism." *Proceedings of the Aristotelian Society* 36: 131–50.

Russell, Bertrand, and Whitehead, Alfred North (1910–13) *Principia Mathematica.* Cambridge University Press, Cambridge.

Sainsbury, Mark and Williamson, Timothy (1995) "Sorites." In Bob Hale and Crispin Wright, eds., *Blackwell Companion to the Philosophy of Language*, Blackwell, Oxford.

Salmon, Nathan U. (1982) *Reference and Essence.* Blackwell, Oxford.

Salmon, Wesley C. (1970) *Zeno's Paradoxes.* Bobbs-Merrill, Indianapolis.

(1980) *Space, Time and Motion: A Philosophical Introduction.* University of Minnesota Press, Minneapolis. 2nd ed.

Sanford, David (1975) "Borderline logic." *American Philosophical Quarterly* 12: 29–39.

(1976) "Competing semantics of vagueness: many values versus super-truth." *Synthese* 33: 195–210.

Savage, C. Wade (1967) "The paradox of the stone." *Philosophical Review* 76: 74–9.

Schlesinger, G. (1974a) *Confirmation and Confirmability*. Oxford University Press, New York.

(1974b) "The unpredictability of free choice." *British Journal for the Philosophy of Science* 25: 209–21.

Schrader, David E. (1979) "A solution to the stone paradox." *Synthese* 42: 255–64.

Scriven, Michael (1951) "Paradoxical announcements." *Mind* 60: 403–7.

Selton, Reinhard (1978) "The chain store paradox." *Theory and Decision* 9: 127–59.

Skyrms, Brian (1975) *Choice and Chance*. Dickenson, Encino, Calif. 2nd ed.

(1982) "Intensional aspects of semantical self-reference." In Martin (1984), pp. 119–31.

Smiley, Timothy (1993) "Can contradictions be true?" *Supplementary Proceedings of the Aristotelian Society* 67: 17–33.

Sorensen, Roy A. (1982) "Recalcitrant variations of the prediction paradox." *Australasian Journal of Philosophy* 60: 355–62.

(1988) *Blindspots*. Clarendon Press, Oxford.

Stack, Michael F. (1977) "A solution to the predictor paradox." *Canadian Journal of Philosophy* 7: 147–54.

Stephanou, Ioannis (1994) "The Meaning of the Logical Constants and the Justification of Logical Laws." University of London PhD thesis.

Storer, Thomas (1961) "MINIAC: World's smallest electronic brain." *Analysis* 22: 151–2.

Strawson, Peter (1950) "On referring." *Mind* 59: 269–86. Reprinted in his *Logico-Linguistic Papers*. Methuen, London. 1971, pp. 1–27.

Tarski, Alfred (1937) "The concept of truth in formalized languages." In his *Logic, Semantics, Metamathematics*. Clarendon Press, New York. 1956, pp. 152–278.

(1969) "Truth and proof." *Scientific American* 194: 63–77.

Thomason, Richmond H. (1970) *Symbolic Logic: An Introduction*. Macmillan, Toronto.

Thomson, James F. (1954) "Tasks and super-tasks." *Analysis* 15: 1–13. Reprinted in Richard M. Gale (1968), pp. 406–21, and in W. C. Salmon (1970), pp. 89–102.

Tye, Michael (1990) "Vague objects." *Mind* 99: 535–57.

(1994a) "Sorites paradoxes and the semantics of vagueness." In James Tomberlin, ed., *Philosophical Perspectives: Logic and Language*. Ridgeview, Atascadero, Calif.

(1994b) "Why the vague need not be higher-order vague." *Mind* 103: 43–5.

Unger, Peter (1979a) "There are no ordinary things." *Synthese* 41: 117–54.

(1979b) "I do not exist." In Graham MacDonald, ed., *Perception and Identity: Essays Presented to A.J. Ayer.* Macmillan, London. 1979, pp. 235–51.

van Fraassen, B. (1966) "Singular terms, truth-value gaps, and free logic." *Journal of Philosophy* 53: 481–5.

(1968) "Presupposition, implication and self-reference." *Journal of Philosophy* 65: 136–52.

van Heijenoort, John (1967) "Logical paradoxes." In Edwards (1967), vol. 5, pp. 44–51.

Vlastos, Gregory (1967) "Zeno of Elea." In Edwards (1967), vol. 8, pp. 369–79.

Wiggins, David (1986) "On singling out an object determinately." In Philip Pettit and John McDowell, eds., *Subject, Thought, and Context.* Oxford University Press, Oxford, pp. 169–80.

Williamson, Timothy (1992a) "Inexact knowledge." *Mind* 101: 218–42.

(1992b) "Vagueness and ignorance." *Supplementary Proceedings of the Aristotelian Society* 66: 145–62.

(1994) *Vagueness.* Routledge, London.

Wittgenstein, Ludwig (1953) *Philosophical Investigations.* Basil Blackwell, Oxford.

Wright, Crispin (1975) "On the coherence of vague predicates." *Synthese* 30: 325–65.

(1976) "Language-mastery and the sorites paradox." In Gareth Evans and John McDowell, eds., *Truth and Meaning.* Oxford University Press, Oxford, pp. 223–47.

(1987). "Further reflections on the sorites paradox." *Philosophical Topics* 15: 227–90.

(1992). "Is higher order vagueness coherent?" *Analysis* 53.3: 129–39.

Wright, Crispin, and Sudbury, Aidan (1977) "The paradox of the unexpected examination." *Australasian Journal of Philosophy* 60: 41–58.

Zadeh, L.A. (1965) "Fuzzy sets." *Information and Control* 8: 338–53.

Index